Untold Stories

Life, Love, and Reproduction

Edited by

Kate Cockrill
Lucia Leandro Gimeno
Steph Herold

ISBN: 1500248517
ISBN 13: 9781500248512
Library of Congress Control Number: 2014911337
CreateSpace Independent Publishing Platform
North Charleston, South Carolina

Book design and illustrations by Mekhi Baldwin www.mekeba-design.com.

Contents

Introduction to Untold Stories

"There is no greater agony than bearing an untold story inside you."

—Maya Angelou

An untold story can be something that we carry with us through our lives, worried about what our friends or families would say if they found out. It can be a story we're desperate to share, hoping that someone will give us a hint that they've[1] been through something similar. Some stories are left untold to protect ourselves or other people we love. Other stories are pushed to the margins, not so much untold as unheard. The pain of carrying an untold story can be deep and sustained or intermittent and surprising. Despite the challenges associated with sharing these stories, it is also true that many of our greatest moments of connection come from being on the receiving end of someone else's untold story.

Perhaps the area of human experience that is most replete with untold stories is that of reproduction. Sexual taboos, gender norms, expectations around ability, and racial prejudices create a world of unwritten rules and proscriptions related to family creation and these rules carry enormous weight. People who transgress these rules are encouraged to remain under the radar, or to interact only with similar folk, and the absence of their stories creates a distorted culture.

"The single story creates stereotypes, and the problem with stereotypes is not that they are untrue,

---

1 We intentionally use they/their/them as a singular pronoun when referring to a person to reflect that some people do not use male or female pronouns nor to assume their gender identity if it is unknown to the writer.

*but that they are incomplete. They make one story
become the only story."*
—Chimamanda Ngozi Adichie

Creating a family, whatever that means to you, is deeply personal and unique. Yet stop anyone on the street and they can tell you a single story of what the "ideal" American family looks like. There are two parents: a cisgender[2] woman and a cisgender man. They are white. They are Christian. They are in their mid-thirties and live in the suburbs. They are upper middle class with comfortable jobs; maybe the mom works, or maybe she doesn't. They had kids exactly when they wanted to—they didn't even need to "try." Maybe they use birth control, or maybe they don't. They certainly don't share the intimate details of their reproductive lives with anyone. It's private.

Yet, if you asked these same people what their *own* families look like, what families in their community look like, you'd get a completely different picture: single parents raising children with friends and extended family; queer families with two gay dads, a lesbian mom with a gender non-conforming[3] partner; two friends deciding to co-parent but not be sexual partners; people choosing not to become parents at all; parents who placed babies or older children for adoption; heterosexual families where one or more parent is trans[*4]; families that are bi- or multiracial; couples that chose to have an abortion and later decided to have children. The stories and experiences would move outward from the narrow American norm in all directions like an exploding star. Too much life to be contained in a single story.

*"Prejudices, it is well known, are most difficult to
eradicate from the heart whose soil has never been*

---

2 The term *cisgender* applies to a person whose gender identity is the same as the gender that was assigned to them at birth.

3 Gender non-conforming: a term used to describe people who do not conform to the gender expectations of their assigned or chosen gender identity.

4 Trans*: a term used to reflect the full spectrum of gender identities that are not cisgender, including transgender, transsexual, genderqueer, genderfluid, non-binary, genderless, agender, non-gendered, non-binary, third gender, two-spirit, bigender, trans man, and trans woman.

*loosened or fertilized by education: they grow there,
firm as weeds among stones."*
—Charlotte Brontë

The problem of untold stories around reproduction occurs on both the demand side and the supply side. On one hand, through our own prejudices and lack of awareness, we often ensure that certain people and stories are left unheard. Many people learn the unwritten rules around family creation as children, and the resulting judgments and prejudices are hard to shake no matter how hard we try. Because creating our own families takes so much strength and sacrifice, it's easy to believe that the way we did things is the way everyone should—that our methods, experiences, and feelings should be universal. Despite our best intentions, we may find ourselves judging our friend who has had children with multiple partners, shaming our cousin who decided to give birth at home instead of in a hospital, and believing that our neighbor who is experiencing infertility deserves it because she's had three abortions. These judgments and prejudices close us off from stories and experiences that may enrich our lives, connect us with people, and challenge our beliefs.

"Shame derives its power from being unspeakable."
—Brené Brown

On the supply side of the untold story problem are experiences of shame and fear.

Deciding to have an abortion, not be a parent, or claim your sexuality are not easy things to do in a world that tells us that we are wrong if we fall outside of the norm. Sometimes, when we form our families in ways we think other people won't understand, we decide to keep secrets, to leave our own stories untold. We think this rational decision will keep us safe from judgment, shame, and misunderstanding.

In all of our lives, there are moments where shame creeps in. Even if the people who raised us gave us the emotional tools and resilience to recover from those moments, we still won't bypass the fear of not being good enough, of not meeting other people's expectations. Often the parts of our lives where there's the most opportunity to create meaning for ourselves are also the parts that are imbued with impossible expectations.

This collection of stories comes from The Sea Change Program, a nonprofit organization committed to a world that upholds the dignity and humanity of all people as they move through their reproductive lives. In this book we seek to address both sides of the single-story problem: the prejudice and the shame. We all have our stones to throw and our closets to bear. This project aims to put people in touch with both sides of themselves simultaneously and explore what happens when we are strong enough to listen and brave enough to share.

The Untold Stories Project: Engaging Reading Circles

"Circles create soothing space, where even reticent people can realize that their voice is welcome."
—Margaret J. Wheatley

We developed The Untold Stories Project based on a simple and often overlooked fact: every circle has untold stories. In 2011 we piloted a first version of this project with people who regularly sit in a circle with one another: book clubs. Advertising our project on Facebook, we reached out as wide as our social networks could carry us. We heard from book clubs in Arkansas, Alabama, California, Maryland, Missouri, New York, New Jersey, and Utah. Fourteen book clubs, including 120 members, signed up for the project, and we shared with them an anthology of true stories about pregnancy, birth, abortion, adoption, miscarriage, infertility, and contraception.

The conversations were rich as participants explored sexual and reproductive taboos, norms, and prejudices, as well as the diverse array of reproductive experiences in the reader and in their own lives. They also learned new things about one another, even if they had known each other for many years. One group discovered that five of their six members had previously had abortions, though none had ever shared these stories in their book club before. Another group explored teen pregnancy through the book and through the experiences of one member who had become a parent at a young age. One book club made up of female members explored how the attitudes of their male partners had shaped their ability to talk about their own reproductive experiences. Another group made up of men discussed how difficult it was to feel fully involved in the reproductive decisions that took place in their own marriages.

In these groups, people reflected on the pain, isolation, and silence that result from keeping our untold stories a secret and the ways that these secrets diminish our ability to connect with one another across experiences and values. Participants noted that the silence and shame surrounding untold stories doesn't just impact the secret-keeper; they saw the consequences in their neighborhoods, communities, and country. They pointed out that stigma creates fertile ground for discriminatory policies, insufficient health-care services, and stereotypical media portrayals.

Reading and discussing untold stories, both their own and the ones they read in the book, brought these readers closer together as a group. They reflected on how shame and fear in sharing their untold stories slowly dissipated over the course of these conversations. Openness and curiosity took hold as members learned more about one another.

The Untold Stories Project: Developing the New Book

The success of our initial project gave us the inspiration to create a unique anthology that explored a broader range of reproductive experiences. In January 2014 we posted an advertisement on Twitter and Facebook seeking new storytellers. We received stories that moved and inspired us. We selected stories based on their ability to provoke discussion and encourage people to connect across different experiences and investigate their own opinions, attitudes and beliefs. All of the initial submissions were from ciswomen; we noted there were no stories by trans* or gender-nonconforming authors. We went to work and did additional outreach. Though this book does not fully reflect our desire to include various trans* and gender-nonconforming perspectives on parenting and abortion, we are glad to have included experiences from straight, queer, trans*, and intersex people.

In developing this collection we aimed to avoid the single story of reproduction and family creation. Yet we know that it runs the risk of reproducing single stories along other lines of identity and experience. Likewise, important stories and perspectives are missing from this book altogether. Though we are proud of this book, we also know that these words are not enough. Our long-term commitment is to lift up voices that go unheard and increase exposure to stories that go untold.

Another commitment we have in this book is to the individuals who have shared their experiences with us. Many of the authors are publishing their work and personal stories for the first time. Their bravery and commitment to changing the single story of reproduction is evident in their writing. But behind the scenes, storytellers shared their own fears that contributing to this reader would invite negative attention or uncomfortable moments. Some authors struggled with going public, and others struggled with their honesty in characterizing their own actions and experiences. Their gift to us is an invitation to experience their stories in all of their perfect imperfection.

The Untold Stories Project: Reading Together

At The Sea Change Program, we call Untold Stories a "project" for a reason. As we noted in our description of the book, this work is incomplete. Without discussion, consideration, and exploration, this collection has no life. This is where you and your circle come in! We invite you to explore and reflect on your own beliefs and views by reading this book with people you know. Like most conversations about personal experiences, we think that exploring this book with good friends and good food will help you get the most out of these stories. We know that when people can sit together and share what they think, know, believe, and have experienced, they feel more connected, open, and engaged.

For some people, the existence of these stories and the culture of shame and silence will come as no surprise. However, this anthology will add context to what we think we know about pregnancy, birth, adoption, infertility, loss, and parenting, exposing readers to stories that have been traditionally on the margins of our society.

Come on this journey with us. Don't be afraid of what you might find. Grab some friends and settle in for a conversation about the things that matter most. And let us know what happens.

Kate Cockrill
Lucia Leandro Gimeno
Steph Herold
The Sea Change Program
untoldstories@seachangeprogram.org

My Bright, Shiny Life of Shame

Karen Harris Thurston

I was thirteen years old when, according to most everyone here in the Deep South, I became a slut and a killer.

That was long ago. I am fifty-four now. Through all these years I have composed whole collections of tomes in my mind, hoping to conjure a magic potion of words that would grant others the willingness to understand and reach a different verdict about me.

As I sit here, my fingers poised over these keys, this white page confronting me, I once again face the immutable fact: Most people in this conservative Christian region never will understand—not even the neighbors, colleagues, and friends I love dearly. Their hearts are kind and their intentions are good, but their minds are made up.

Only a woman with a life like mine would understand, a woman who has spent decades terrified that others—including her own husband and children—will discover her past and abandon her in disgust. I've never met such a woman, but I know she is close by in this middle-class suburb where I am a wife, mother, and teacher's assistant in a kindergarten classroom.

She is so near, in fact, that we've probably bumped carts in the supermarket or sat next to each other at our kids' soccer games. There are millions of us, yet we are grand masters at hiding in plain sight, gold medalists at social camouflage, and so we remain strangers to this day.

She would understand everything, even if I never opened up my heart and poured out the thick mix of circumstances that produced the foundation of my identity—the accidental pregnancies that I ended at the ages of thirteen and nineteen.

We would tell each other every detail anyway, just to release what we've locked in our hearts and minds for so long. However, now that we are in the second half-centuries of our lives, facing into our sunset years, we would not linger long on the stories of our unplanned conceptions. Two tall glasses of sweet tea later and we'd be moving on to the truly afflictive theme of our lives.

Our stories are no longer about the pregnancies we stopped. They are about what it means to live in coerced psychological isolation amid everlasting mental and emotional punishment here in the Bible Belt.

Our stories have a beautiful bright side. We were born into middle-class white families. We could afford and access legal reproductive health-care services that existed through the efforts of compassionate people who understood the real lives of girls and women. We had the freedom and the means to make wrenching but morally responsible decisions in times of crisis.

We were able to pursue basic human happiness, to reach for the dreams common to all humankind—to get educations, work in fulfilling jobs, nurture stable families, and forge healthy, loving relationships. Millions of other girls and women—for no good reason other than being born into different circumstances—were deprived of reproductive health care and denied options. They faced the ruinous devastation of their hopes and aspirations, but we were spared.

This gift of privilege renders me morally duty-bound to help improve the future for the little girls of today. I have such scant power, but it's just enough to generate a flicker of light that I can shine into the dark force that underlies every injustice, every cruelty that girls and women confront in their reproductive lives. I can tell my story of stigma—how it entered my world and consumed it like kudzu, how I coped with the raw fear it provoked, and how compassionate people helped me overcome it.

Maybe the best place to begin is in church in the sweet summertime of childhood. I was about eight years old when I heard our minister preach about Christ's call to turn the other cheek. The memory is vivid not because of his eloquence or the superhero aura of his black robe, but because of what happened later—an event that foreshadowed my future.

I skipped out of the house, the screen door slamming behind me, and headed to the playground, following a dirt path that snaked around the edge of a pond. I stopped to admire the cattails, their velvety stalks ringed with little assemblies of dragonflies.

Then I saw two boys on the opposite shore. They squatted at the water's edge, their bare feet sunk into the dark mud. They leaned their heads together, fixing their eyes on me as they whispered. The enchantment of the afternoon vanished.

The boys began to laugh wickedly. Like a strange species of waterfowl stirring to take flight, they sprang up and whirled their arms in broad circles. I felt a *thud* on my shirt, a heavy *thump* on my head, and stings like needles pricking the bare skin of my face and arms. They were bombarding me with mud.

But I was fresh from the sanctuary, filled with faith in Jesus, so I did not run. Instead, I turned to present my cheek in all of its freckled glory. As the mud kept raining down, I began to wonder how the savior would rescue me from my enemies as the preacher had promised. I recall looking up at the blue heavens, hoping he might appear like Superman.

Finally, I bolted. I can still feel how my hair, all clumped and matted, slapped like ropes at my face as I fled. I ran until I was choked for breath, until cramps pierced my sides, hot tears of humiliation rolling in dirty streams down my cheeks.

This is what stigma feels like, only the mud is made of messages that strike at the heart and mind. The malicious and unwarranted messages never stop. They keep flying out of every corner of everyday life, but there is nowhere to run for refuge. Inwardly, I am ever dripping in their muck; outwardly, I am ever turning to present my freckled cheek.

My troubles started when I was born a female, but the inequities of our gender are self-evident. So I'll jump ahead to the 1970s, when I failed in spectacular fashion at the game of life. This game, a sport in which all the rules have been written by human and heavenly men, is rigged against us. The object for males is conquest—to have sex early, often, and by any means possible. The males almost always win, and they have nothing to lose. The object for females is purity. They must refuse all male advances—be they gentlemanly, aggressive, or violent—until marriage. The females rarely win, and they have absolutely everything to lose, from their self-respect to their reputations to their promising futures.

My first failure was as a freshman in high school. I was uneducated about sex and worn down by a boyfriend who was a senior. The physical pain of it was horrifying. One day I woke up with an illness so odd that I told everyone about it, including the principal. I can see myself approaching his barrel chest in the hall, the gray lockers aligned around us like uniformed witnesses. As we passed each other, he asked how I was doing. I babbled on and on: *It's so strange. I throw up in the morning, but I feel fine after I eat. Isn't that so weird?*

My parents made arrangements without discussion. We had a single conversation in which they swore me to secrecy for the rest of my days. We never spoke of it again—not of the events leading up to it, not of the fallout afterward. Their world proceeded as before, but mine was never the same. I knew that girls have only two social ranks here in the South: good or bad. Once a girl is bad, she is bad for good.

The second failure was with an aspiring pilot who treated me terribly. I was prepared to marry him and become a mother, but he dropped me off at the clinic instead. I was filled with a primal sense of relief as I awaited his return to drive me home. Time passed. The lobby emptied, the phones hushed, and the receptionist tidied the coffee-table magazines. The clinic was closing, she said. *Are you sure you have a ride?* I had only one certainty. I was profoundly and terrifyingly alone, regardless.

My humiliation was so heavy that I could barely rise from the chair. I stood up and moved as if through syrup, down the hall and out into the blinding sunlight. I wandered back and forth, traveling what seemed like many miles over the cracked and weedy sidewalk. In the roar of passing traffic, gusts of fumes flew at me from the street like shoves.

All these years later, my heart aches for the frightened young woman I was then, still living at home, panicked that her parents would learn the truth. I can see her as day after day she enters her bedroom closet. She closes the door quietly and sinks to the floor, writhing and sobbing under the hems of her dresses, her face in a pillow to mute the anguish. I watch her riding the city bus, turning her face to the window, discreetly blotting tears with a tissue in her fist. Here she is in the library, taking the elevator to a sparsely visited floor, meandering through the stacks to a secluded study carrel. She sits for hours before an open book feigning to read, catching tears in Kleenex.

I could not go on, yet I carried on. The months collected into years, and the years gathered into decades. I finished college, worked as a journalist, married, raised two children, volunteered in my community, became an educator in the public schools. Yet all was not as bright and shiny as it seemed.

A steady stream of stigma has been pouring into my world, polluting it with cruel messages of shame and fear. It has been piped into every nook and cranny of my day-to-day life through all manner of media—radios and televisions, magazines and newspapers, billboards and bumper stickers. The flow of shame is especially heavy during election cycles, when conservative candidates rally their Christian base around the female reproductive system.

Most of the stigma I experience originates with religious institutions and pious individuals who deliberately engineer it, hoping disgrace and fear will stop girls and women from using safe, legal reproductive health care. This calculated intimidation forces compassionate people into terrified silence, allowing the menace of stigma to thrive. In the public schools, we call this bullying.

The steady drone of overt social shame is so ubiquitous it's become mere background noise to people who never have and never will experience a reproductive crisis. But the hectoring messages come to me as if through a bullhorn pressed to my ear. No place is safe, and no time of day is exempt from the self-righteous voice of shame.

I'm at home in my family room at dinnertime, eating chicken potpie and watching a disaster flick from the 1970s called *Airport*. In an early cockpit scene, the pilot mentions he has fathered seven children. The copilot stammers something like, *What about the unplanned ones? Did you ever think of doing something about them, before they were born?* The response: *Of course not! The ones that were not planned are the most special children of all.*

I'm riding bikes with a colleague on a spring weekend. We're pedaling through sun-dappled neighborhoods, chatting about work and motherhood, when she brings up her minister and his spirited evangelism on the evils of ending pregnancies.

I'm at a dinner party where a young man rakes a cracker through the spinach dip while recalling his stellar performance in a college debate class. The topic was about women ending unintended pregnancies. *As a Christian I'm passionately against it,* he says, *so it was very easy to argue my case.*

I'm chaperoning a class of first-graders on a field trip to an auditorium at a private school where young teens are putting on a play about Pocahontas. Near the entrance is a garden of ferns, their tendrils pointing like arrows to a marble statue with an inscription about saving the unborn.

I'm standing on a ladder, hot-gluing a giant number line to a wall as I help a new teacher set up her classroom. She talks of her religious faith and, because an election looms, she announces that she cannot abide women who end pregnancies.

I'm driving to the grocery store, stopping at a red light behind an SUV. The dark glass of the back window is salted with cheery cartoon stickers representing the family ensconced within. The fender sports a familiar bumper sticker proclaiming God's stance on women's reproductive rights and the calculated implication that women like me are cheerleaders of death.

I'm sitting on the commode in the restroom at work. Someone has placed a stack of celebrity magazines on the little table that holds the air freshener and a pyramid of toilet paper. The glossy issue on top features a national politician and her teenage daughter, both grinning and cuddling infants under the headline *We're Glad We Chose Life.*

I'm rolling down the interstate with my family, heading to a world-famous theme park for vacation. A giant Jesus comes into view on a billboard about fetal heartbeats. Minutes later, the billboard appears again. Further on, there it is once more. Mile after mile, the same billboard of shame keeps up its harassment like a stalker. It's as if the drive to Orlando is an approach to a women's health-care clinic. The interstate is like a sidewalk lined with protesters—persecutors, actually—screaming accusations of baby murder at distressed girls and women.

I'm in my classroom, helping orchestrate an annual indoor picnic lunch. The teacher turns on the TV and surfs for the school's closed-circuit station showing a film about the pilgrims. In a fleeting moment, the TV passes through a religious program, just long enough for the words *killing babies* to come sailing out over my head as I open a child's carton of chocolate milk.

As these messages of shame accrue inside the mind, undiluted by any counterpoints of compassion, they create an inner climate ripe for self-recrimination. Innocuous situations unfold in which the mental muck stirs up. For example, I'm in line to donate blood, filling out the requisite paperwork, when my eyes rest upon the question *How many pregnancies have you had?*

Through all the years of social shaming, I did not regret that I had been able to turn to a compassionate and legal health-care option. Rather, the stigma provoked other kinds of mental and emotional torment— self-loathing and terror. I hated myself for the twists and turns that had brought me to those desperate situations when I was young. And I lived in fear, not only of God's wrath, but also of complete alienation from the human family.

I'd watch my sons riding their tricycles in the driveway, or see them waving to me from their used cars as they drove off to college, or picture them flying across the country for job interviews, and I always wondered if this would be the time that God would take them from me through a fatal crash. I always waited upon the Lord's vengeance. Also, I believed my sons' hearts would harden against me if they ever learned of my past. What a cruel and vindictive belief to have hammered into your deepest consciousness.

Every caring relationship I ever formed felt imperiled by a menacing conviction: *If they really knew me, they would despise me.* My husband would seek a divorce. The neighbors would turn their backs. My colleagues would walk a wide berth. The parents of the boys and girls I nurture in my class-room would yank their children from my hugs.

At times the messages of shame and fear trigger physical reactions. My heart might suddenly race, or quiver in my chest, or sink to my feet, or leap to my throat. Sometimes I have the sensation of straining to breathe. It's like walking around with my mind in an invisible cloud of toxic gas. Even the word *abortion* sparks involuntary physical reflexes. Its vowels and consonants have melded over time into a weapon studded with spikes and blades, like one of Q's inventions in a James Bond film. I flee from the word as if I am a fugitive from the law and it is a police siren.

Throughout my life I have dabbled with various coping strategies. I wrote down thoughts and feelings. I drank too heavily and too often. I devoured self-help books. I walked and biked for miles to work out the distress. I mentored adolescent girls. And I built a mental wall of numbness around my inner world, like a Plexiglas tunnel in a tourist aquarium.

On all sides I see the sharks and piranhas circle, yet I smile cheerfully through my day-to-day life.

Another strategy was to build up my Christian faith, so I immersed myself in church life. I became a lay minister, taught vacation Bible school, cooked food for the needy, attended worship services twice weekly. Most important of all, I spent a year reading the Bible from beginning to end. After that, I wanted to tell the good news to everyone, like this: I pull into a parking spot next to a car with a bumper sticker that says *God is pro-life*. A woman gets out and hurries toward her destination. I grab my Bible and leap out of my car, beseeching her to wait. I apologize breathlessly for bothering her. *But I couldn't help noticing your bumper sticker,* I say. She glances at my Bible and smiles. *Well, here's the thing,* I continue. *You cannot possibly be aware of what it really says in here. Wait till you hear this.* And then I read the myriad scriptures in which God calls for the slaughter of infants and children.

This scenario is a fantasy, of course. I would not try to argue people out of their religious beliefs. But reading the Bible—thinking critically about its content, its origins, and its use through antiquity to manipulate and condition human behavior—empowered me to stand up for myself in my mind. Imaginings like this, in which I face my attackers, have helped arrest my habit of beating myself up.

Another miracle graced my life in church. I met a new friend—a minister's daughter ten years my senior. One summer day we went for a fateful walk. Down a red clay road we traveled, our voices mingling with the trilling of sparrows on fence posts. It seemed like a simple summer stroll, until she made a startling confession. She had become pregnant in her teens. Her parents had sent her away to live out her pregnancy and then arranged an adoption. Years later she tried in vain to find the child.

Here was a woman who understood an accidental pregnancy, who knew the anguish of shame rooted in religion. My heart began to thrash against my ribs as my forbidden truth, caged in my mind for so long, came winging out of my mouth. I felt insanely terrified, as if I had pulled the pin from a grenade that I could not toss. I waited for an explosion, for the earth to swallow me. But the cicadas continued to hum and the butterflies kept up their airborne ballet. We walked on, sharing everything, without the need to justify or rationalize anything. At forty years of age, I experienced blessed love, compassion, and understanding for the very first time. This love gave me the courage to slowly venture out of my inner prison.

Two years later I told my husband. He did not flee in disgust. He listened, learned, held me in his arms, and became my greatest supporter on my journey to "come out" and to advocate for reproductive health and rights.

Eight months ago, I shared my history with my grown sons—the children whose lives are owed to the precise unfolding of my youth. If I had become a mother in my teens, these young men would not be here, serving in medical and transportation careers, preparing to raise families of their own.

My sons did not reject me. They listened, learned, and understood. They embraced me. One spoke these words now etched on my heart: *Mom, I loved you yesterday. I love you now. And I will love you tomorrow.* The other took my hand and walked me into the world of social media, where I was stunned to discover that millions of caring people are working around the globe on all fronts of reproductive health care and rights. I felt like Dorothy, stepping out of the gray, battered house of my mind into a strange, dazzling, beautiful place of compassion.

This is how I can believe that God is love and that love is kind. My husband, children, and close friends still love me. They do not believe I am a slut and a killer. They do not believe I need forgiveness for being human. The worst fears contrived by all the religious heckling in my life did not materialize.

As I make these final keystrokes, I confess that I am still scared. But I am resolved. I will not allow shame and fear to rule my life anymore. In my mind, I am already saying farewell to people I expect will shun me. I forgive them.

No longer will I be complicit in the silence that allows stigma to flourish. I will stand up straight and speak out with dignity, because nothing matters more to me now than the future of the little girls I see each day.

They approach me in the classroom bearing construction-paper bouquets of daisies and tulips, sketched in bright crayon under skies of rainbows and butterflies. As they leave my hugs and return to their desks, their ponytails swaying, their light-up sneakers sparkling, the prayers of my heart follow them: *May they never be taught to see themselves as deflowered. May they never be taught to believe they are killers. May they live in a compassionate world that grants them the divine human right of complete reproductive justice.*

———

Karen Harris Thurston is a teacher's assistant in a public elementary school in metro Atlanta. For two decades she has helped young students develop self-confidence and a love of learning. She is a former newspaper reporter and freelance writer with a master's degree in journalism from the University of Georgia. She has been married to her best friend for thirty years, and they have two grown sons, a daughter-in-law, and a pair of rescued dogs. A former lay minister, Karen has served as a hospital volunteer, teen mentor, literacy tutor, and public speaker for Mothers Against Drunk Driving.

Story Reflection Questions

1. What is one moment in the story that stayed with you?

   _____

   _____

   _____

2. What questions did you find yourself asking as you read the story?

   _____

   _____

   _____

3. What challenged you about the story?

   _____

   _____

   _____

4. What surprised you about the story?

   _____

   _____

   _____

5. How does this story relate to your own life experience?

   _____

   _____

   _____

Unplanned

Malkia Hutchinson

I have always admired women who were capable of raising their children on their own. My own mother was single, and, even if I wasn't fully cognizant of her struggles and sacrifices at the time, I appreciated the magnitude of what that meant. As much as I was in awe of what it meant to parent a child or children while living apart from the other parent, I wholeheartedly believed single parenthood was a fate meant for other types of women and nothing that would ever become a part of my life. I had done everything "right": I excelled in school, graduated from Cornell University, joined the Peace Corps, and worked at a prominent community health center in Washington, DC. I was planning out my life while also taking time to enjoy my new community in a dynamic city.

During the winter of 2010, I met someone at a friend's going-away party. He was friendly, and I could tell he was into me, but I wasn't as interested in him at the time. That night, he was kind enough to drive me around as I was attempting to meet up with other friends; when those plans eventually fell through, however, I decided to go to the housewarming party he was missing in order to spend time with me. Over the course of the next few weeks, we went on a few dates. and, with a bit of persuasion on his end, we committed to being in a monogamous relationship. The official boyfriend/girlfriend label was adopted the following April, and in August I took several over-the-counter pregnancy tests that all came back positive. I had known something wasn't right but had attributed my sluggishness, nausea, and mild headache to something I must have picked up from a recent trip overseas.

But there I was, standing in front of four pregnancy tests that finally confirmed to me what I felt in the depths of my being was the cause of my feeling just a little "off." My boyfriend was not at all pleased.

"Are you sure?" he asked as he sat next to me on his bed.

"Yeah, I'm pretty sure. I took a few tests."

He looked almost baffled as he said, "I can't believe this is happening again."

I didn't follow up on that, since my own mind was a blur. Later, he admitted to me that this wasn't his first experience with unplanned pregnancy. The thought of termination crossed both of our minds. After talking to two close friends over the phone, and clinging to the hope that at-home pregnancy tests aren't as reliable as a doctor's visit, I made an appointment with my gynecologist. Several days later it was confirmed, yet again, that I was most definitely pregnant.

The term *crisis pregnancy* was something I said often during my college days as an antiabortion advocate. It was both a state of being and a situation I felt I understood by virtue of wanting to provide abortion alternatives to pregnant women. I volunteered at a crisis pregnancy center (CPC), convinced I was playing a vital role in persuading women to choose life for their unborn children. The word *crisis* doesn't seem to capture the sensation of being pregnant when you don't want to be by a boyfriend you've known for less than six months. The feelings of terror, hopelessness, fear, and shame kept washing over me. He saw termination as the only logical solution. He never stopped talking about it. I went to a local CPC with a friend, where they didn't tell me anything I didn't expect them to. I knew they would show me colorful pictures of five-week-old fetuses and talk about the wonderful services they could provide. I knew the few things they were offering would be very temporary, but it was the first glimpse of tangible support I felt since finding out I was pregnant.

I visited the Planned Parenthood several blocks away from where I worked just to have someone I could talk to who didn't have an agenda. The woman I sat with was amazing. We talked about my relationship with my boyfriend, family, job, goals, and the future I saw for myself. "What would prevent you from reaching those goals if you continued this pregnancy?" she asked.

"Well," I started, "for one thing, I doubt I'm going to marry my boyfriend. I can see how this situation would lead me to become a single mom. I can't go to graduate school and pursue the career I want if I'm a single mom."

Without prodding me much further, she talked to me about her sister's journey through single motherhood and all that she had been able to accomplish after having a child at nineteen. We also discussed the possibility of moving home to be closer to family and the fact that I adore children and have always wanted to be a mother. I left knowing I wouldn't be able to go through with an abortion. I knew I'd be continuing my pregnancy and had to stand firmly in that decision with my boyfriend.

As I anticipated, he wasn't happy with my decision. "How is this even going to work?" he exclaimed. "We don't have family here, and all of our friends are our age and have lives and jobs of their own. They're not going to be able to help us."

All legitimate points, but I insisted that we could find a way to make it work. He went to the first sonogram appointment but was emotionless. It was after this first ultrasound, where he barely looked at me and wouldn't hold my hand, that we sat in a coffee shop and he dejectedly told me, "I just don't understand why you can't get the abortion." In retrospect, I can sympathize with him. As a young black man just beginning his career, the last thing he wanted was to become someone's "baby daddy." He rose out of an environment endemic with baby mamas, baby daddies, and fatherlessness. He wanted better for himself.

Throughout my pregnancy, the shame and stigma of being a black woman with a swollen belly yet no ring on *that* finger grew and consumed me. Nobody could see my resume beyond any of that. It was incredibly difficult to feel happy or excited about the miraculous thing my body was doing. I went through the first half of my pregnancy in a daze. I'm not sure what caused me to snap out of it, but I remember feeling disconnected with my ob-gyn care. There were no providers of color and it was a really large practice. There was no guarantee that the person I saw for my routine care would be the person present for my delivery. In fact, since she was a nurse practitioner, she wouldn't be the one delivering my child.

I discussed some of these concerns with a coworker who was in a similar situation. She got pregnant after a one-night stand and went through the pregnancy and delivery without the support of the child's father. She also went through the ob-gyn practice I was in and validated many of my apprehensions. Over lunch one day, she mentioned watching the film *The Business of Being Born* toward the end of her pregnancy but wished she had found it earlier. On her recommendation, I viewed the movie as well and realized that I could have other options for a birth aside from what I had grown accustomed to. I didn't *have* to deliver in a hospital. That was an incredibly empowering realization for me during a time when I felt like my power was being sapped out of me day by day. I went back and forth about where I would live when my lease was up. At that point I would be twenty weeks pregnant. I wouldn't be able to afford to live on my own, so my choices were either to move in with my child's father or move back home. He and I ended up moving in together, but our relationship never fully recovered. He stayed out late and cheated on me with other women, leaving me at home, growing resentful and depressed.

"I don't see why you even bothered to move in with me if you had no desire to be faithful to me or be around when I need you," I'd shout in frustration.

"You gave me an ultimatum and told me either we had to live together or you'd move home and have the baby there!" he responded, which only led to more yelling, screaming, and aggravation.

I had no family in the area and felt like I had no other option than to endure it, with the hope that the baby's arrival would change things for the better. Even though I was a passenger in my relationship, I was in control of how this baby was going to transition earth-side. The fact that I was beginning to take ownership of my body and my birthing experience was critical for me during that time.

I began to dread the trips to the doctor's office. Feeling out of place as the only black woman in the waiting room was one thing, but I never felt completely comfortable being an unmarried black woman in a practice that seemed to draw married white women dressed like they had just walked over from their lobbying firms. I honestly believe I was not treated differently by the front-desk staff or my provider compared to these women, but I wanted to see other women who looked like me providing my medical care. I also knew I wanted to work with a midwife and didn't want to give birth in a hospital. These realizations left me with very few options.

There was a well-regarded midwifery practice out of George Washington University Hospital that met my new midwifery requirement, but since it was in a hospital it didn't appeal to me. Then I came across a stand-alone birth center located in Northeast DC. It was purposely built in a low-income, predominately black area of the city due to that population's poor maternal health outcomes. I loved the intentionality behind that.

I visited the birth center and immediately fell in love. The birthing suites were beautiful and homey. The staff was incredibly friendly. The midwives and breastfeeding peer supporters, all women of color, were very welcoming. I could tell these women loved the work they were doing in the community. What I didn't count on was my reaction to the women who were in the waiting area and in my tour group. My desire to be around people who looked more like me and shared a similar cultural background gave way to a feeling of discomfort at being with women who appeared uneducated and had multiple children by multiple men.

I felt frustrated that I didn't belong anywhere. I didn't belong in the predominately white medical practice that would have me birth in a hospital where my movements would be restricted and I couldn't eat, drink, or do what my body was telling me to do as I birthed my child. But how did I fit in this environment with women of color who seemed disinterested in breastfeeding, hadn't pursued higher education, and faced yet another unplanned pregnancy while their other children were still in diapers?

This experience was yet another illustration of my life growing up not "black enough" in this space and not "white enough" in that space. Every time I opened my mouth, my speech gave me away as someone who didn't belong in that community. I may have looked the part, but my internalized classism kept rearing its ugly head as I mulled over making the decision of whether to switch practices. However, I knew I wanted to be with a practice that embraced, not just tolerated, intervention-free birth. Ultimately I committed to the birth center, which meant my prenatal care would look drastically different.

The midwives used a group care model, which meant that all women due in the same month were in prenatal classes together. Every other week we came together to discuss breastfeeding, wearing our babies in carriers, changing diapers, our fears and expectations, and to make belly casts and check in with our midwives. It was radically different from what I was used to. I weighed myself and took my own blood pressure, handled and read through my own chart, and got genuine one-on-one time with my provider. I also got to know the other women whom I would have otherwise written off. They were clever, funny, had hands-on parenting advice, were invested in their futures and their children's futures, and, most like myself, appreciated the support and care they received at our birth center. Many of them had previous birthing experiences that bordered on traumatic: doctors who refused to listen to them, episiotomies they had explicitly stated they did not want, and other interventions given without knowing the effects these could have on their labors and bodies.

I had great conversations with these women. One young woman had a thirteen-month-old daughter and was due with a boy in April. She explained, "I never meant to get pregnant right after having my first kid, and I'm really disappointed in myself. But I try not to beat myself up over it too much. I have to be strong for both of my babies."

I was also forced to check respectability politics I hadn't known I subscribed to but occasionally crept into my visits in this environment. If I'm honest with myself, as great as it was to have this space dedicated to the health and well-being of moms and babies situated within an underserved community, I felt like I was still different from "them." In reality, I feared becoming "them." I feared having to maneuver through a crowded bus with a baby instead of relying on private transportation. I feared the thoughts that would surely be running through the minds of my daughter's friends' parents when they realized that I was just another unmarried black woman with a kid. I didn't want to perpetuate the destruction of the black family with my body and choices. I didn't want my child to grow up without a father present in the home as I had. It didn't matter that I was a positive statistic by many measures (educated, healthy, career-driven) because I wasn't married. I was choosing to bring my child into a broken home. I didn't want the world to see me in the same way that I saw "those women" waiting in the lobby with their babies, those women going to prenatal and pediatrician appointments without their children's father, those women without rings on *that* finger.

Shame can be debilitating. It can keep you in an unhealthy and destructive relationship in which your mental, emotional, and physical well-being are inconsequential. It can isolate you. It can cause you to become dependent upon people and relationships you have no business being dependent upon. In the midst of my shame at my out-of-wedlock pregnancy, I found solace in those biweekly, and eventually weekly, visits to my birth center.

What I assumed were Braxton-Hicks contractions woke me up around two o'clock in the morning a week before my daughter was due. Shortly thereafter my water broke, marking the beginning of a twenty-hour labor and delivery. The majority of this happened at home. In the weeks building up to this moment, my child's father vacillated between interest in preparing our home for the baby and a desire to be free from the situation. While most of our preparation tasks had been completed, a few had not, like installing the car seat and putting together the changing table. Our parents were set to fly in the following week, which was when she was due. That night it was only us in our home, and he was busy putting together the changing table (I had freaked out that it wasn't finished yet). I timed my contractions and comforted myself. I rolled on the labor ball by myself, listened to music, and just did the best I could to bear the pain as much as possible.

When we finally got to the birth center, I was nine centimeters dilated, throwing up, and ready for it to all be over. I can't remember how, but I eventually got into a bathtub full of warm water, which my body was craving. I was told to do what my body wanted. My body wanted the Jacuzzi bubbles on and off at intermittent times. It wanted to lie back as the waves passed over me. I'd planned to be surrounded by friends as I welcomed my child earth-side. But in that moment of labor all I wanted were dim lights and quiet. Finally, my body wanted to push.

I can't remember the pain in the way that most women can't remember their labor pains. I do remember my baby being placed on my chest, looking up at me, and me thinking, "It's you!" as if I'd always known her, as if she was who I was expecting. It was miraculous and perfect. It didn't occur to me at that point what I didn't have: mainly a stable relationship with her father, let alone a marriage. I was just consumed by what I had. I had gotten myself through labor mainly by using the techniques I'd picked up at this birth center—this space that was radical in its presence within this community, teaching mostly women of color that their bodies, birth, and babies matter, that you can listen to your body while giving birth and, after birth, breastfeed for as long as you please, that our bodies during pregnancy are phenomenal vessels to be listened to and respected, not problems to be solved.

My journey into parenthood after my daughter's birth has been rocky and, unfortunately, not without moments of shame and sadness. I stayed with her father until she was about eight months old. A final act of violation against my body and spirit was enough to finally send me back home to Texas. Nine months of unemployment and a year of living at home often left me feeling discouraged and unfulfilled. I went through waves of feeling like a failure and as if I'd thrown away a promising future. I eventually landed a position at a women's resource center on a university campus in Houston. Moving south from the Dallas/Ft. Worth area was a huge leap of faith. I don't have family here and didn't know many people before moving down. But my child and I have made a good life for ourselves down here. She's doing very well in her toddler Spanish immersion class and will be moving to the preschool program over the summer.

I have always had a goal of getting a master's degree and worried about how that would play out as a single parent. Before I got pregnant, I was set on studying public health and had no intention of doing so south of the Mason-Dixon line. However, my interest in politics and public policy intensified after I returned to Texas. In the wake of increased legislative efforts to restrict reproductive health options for women in our state and in researching public education options for my child, I felt drawn more to social policy than public health. Incidentally, the university I work at has a master's in public administration program with a policy track that appealed to me. I'm now enrolled in my first semester and will hopefully be able to graduate in two and a half years.

I'm by no means fully secure in my identity as a black single mother. But I recognize that I've accomplished so much and have grown by leaps and bounds. My daughter, Araiya, is a phenomenal child who never ceases to delight me. I'm a great mommy to her, and we're an amazingly strong family unit. Everything else can take a backseat while I continue working to make both of our lives better from here on out.

Malkia Hutchinson grew up in Arlington, Texas, and graduated from Cornell University with a degree in sociology. Between her junior and senior years, Malkia also worked in a domestic violence shelter in Texas. Working in this role, along with feminist, gender, and sexuality studies courses she was enrolled in, led her to a deeper interest in intersectional feminism. She served two years in the Peace Corps as an HIV health educator in Swaziland. Upon her return to the United States, she started working as a community health educator in Washington, DC, for a nonprofit health center that focuses on HIV/AIDS issues. She now serves as the program director of the University of Houston Women's Resource Center while also working toward a master's in public administration. Though she's new to Houston, she's slowly falling in love with its vibrant activist community. Malkia is the proud mother of Araiya, a bright and hilarious three-year-old who won't stop singing songs from *Frozen*.

Story Reflection Questions

1. What is one moment in the story that stayed with you?

_____

_____

_____

2. What questions did you find yourself asking as you read the story?

_____

_____

_____

3. What challenged you about the story?

_____

_____

_____

4. What surprised you about the story?

_____

_____

_____

5. How does this story relate to your own life experience?

_____

_____

_____

A Map for Lost Birth Mothers

Angelique Miste Saavedra

June 2009: Unexpectedly Expecting

For about a week I couldn't stop blaming the soulful singer Erykah Badu and my new favorite song of hers, "The Healer." She wasn't directly responsible, but throughout my first years in college I developed a justifiable crush on her musical brilliance. In a fit of desperation to see her perform live, I invited my musician ex-boyfriend to a festival she'd be performing at. I had met him about a year earlier in a used bookstore, and our relationship had been the definition of unstable ever since. I reassured myself that even though our relationship was finally over, he was a musician and none of my other friends would appreciate Badu the same way he would. Inevitably spending time with my ex during the music festival reignited good memories from our past relationship, and we slept together.

After the festival I promised myself that, for my own dignity, I'd stop seeing my ex. A little over a month after I made that decision, it was too late. One night I found myself alone, curled into a ball, and crying, two positive pregnancy tests sitting in front of me. The timing of this unexpected news couldn't have been worse, as I was about to leave the country for a summer volunteer trip to Northern Africa. It was a trip for which I had been saving and planning for months. Upon discovering my pregnancy, I felt paralyzed by a reality I couldn't accept, convinced my life was over.

Planned Parenthood was the inevitable next step. When they confirmed my pregnancy, I slipped out of my body and watched as my face
became pale. I burst into tears after a staff member calmly asked, "So,
would you like to have an abortion, choose adoption, or parent?" I didn't
realize such a simple question could feel so complicated, and I shriveled up
at the thought of making a decision. I needed time to process everything.
A week wasn't enough, and I didn't want to travel to another continent
after receiving an abortion, especially because my part-time job offered me
no medical insurance. And so I left for Northern Africa carrying not only
my luggage, but the weight of a difficult choice.

September 2009: Choices

Upon my return to the United States, I needed to make a decision. I had
spent about two months away, and although I was scared out of my mind, I
decided not to have an abortion. It was a difficult decision and one that I had
the privilege of putting a lot of thought into. However, this delicate choice
didn't mean I planned on parenting my child. Despite deciding to carry the
pregnancy to term, I knew that I was not ready to be a mother, and I was
curious about how open adoption could be a potential solution for me.

There was an adoption agency I had my eye on, and I immediately
contacted them. After getting a feel for my situation, they eagerly mailed
me a mountain of information. Their brochures advertised birth mothers
glowing and smiling down at their big bellies. The adoptive parents pictured were blissfully united with their babies. Beautifully written thank-
you letters to the adoption agency from both adoptive and birth parents
were common throughout the booklets. It was everything I needed to
confirm that adoption was the best decision for me.

A few weeks later, I received hard-copy profiles of prospective adoptive
parents. They were each designed and created by the couples themselves, so
their personalities showed through the pages. I was giddy at the thought of
my child's future with one of these amazing couples. I took the time to flip
through all of the unique profiles and smiled at the diverse array of families
and hopeful couples.

My ex-boyfriend agreed to meet me at a café so he could look at the profiles of potential adoptive parents. Overall, he was hesitant about adoption but assured me that he would support my decision. Together we arranged the profiles according to our preferences in the hopes of finding a couple we could both agree on.

October 2009: My Baby's Mama

There was one potential adoptive couple in particular whom we placed at the top of our list. They were both college-educated professional artists and led a healthy lifestyle. Most importantly, they were multiracial. My child would be a quarter Mexican, a quarter African American, and half white. I needed the potential adoptive couple to understand what it meant to have curly hair and to raise a child who would experience the world as a person of color. I told my case manager at the adoption agency that I was interested in meeting them and having them be the parents of my child.

A few days later, I received a voice message from the potential adoptive mother. She sounded bubbly and genuinely enthusiastic at the prospect of meeting me. I called her back immediately to set a date to meet her and her husband. I remember wanting to jump up and down for joy.

My ex-boyfriend and I borrowed a friend's car to meet the potential adoptive parents for dinner. When we arrived, they greeted me with hugs, smiles, and gifts. At the time I was so grateful that they had gone through the trouble of making me a gift basket and writing me a thoughtful note. There was an instant spark. We talked about their dreams of having a child, their experiences with infertility, and how excited they were to learn that I was interested in them as parents for my child. After the initial meeting, I felt lucky to have chosen such a kind and loving couple.

What I couldn't tell the adoptive couple was that before dinner, my ex and I had had a huge fight. In the car, he told me he didn't want to meet them, and he ignored my attempts at discussion by blasting loud music.

After dinner, I eagerly awaited his reaction. By the time we walked out of the restaurant, his mood had completely shifted. He felt very happy about the meeting with the potential adoptive parents and said they were great. I was relieved to hear his positive response, especially considering the huge argument we had had before meeting them.

November 2009: The Pregnant Student

"How exciting!" A fellow student in my statistics class had just noticed that my stomach had recently expanded. I gulped. I knew I wasn't ready for her next question. "Have you decided on any names?"

"Uh, Harmony…" I managed to offer. This was the name that I gave my unborn daughter.

"How beautiful! Are you going to take some time off of school?" She had a look of concern plastered on her face.

Another gulp. "No, that won't be necessary." We had a statistics final exam approaching, and I was doing my best to maintain my focus on not only nourishing the growing child, but my own student brain.

She smiled. "When is your due date?"

"February eighth," I stated flatly with a hint that I wasn't interested in answering any more of her questions. My heart couldn't afford to break during statistics class.

After my daily round of classes ended, I took the bus back home. Throughout my first months of pregnancy, I endured an overwhelming amount of morning sickness. As my pregnancy progressed, the nausea diminished, but I'd still suffer from motion sickness on the bumpy bus ride home.

The most excruciating memories from those bus rides were people's strange and distant glares. Granted, some smiled warmly at my growing tummy, but most stares felt icy cold. I could sense the strangers' judgments sinking beneath my skin simply because of what I appeared to be: a young Hispanic single mother-to-be, dependent on public transportation. Taking the bus always made me feel vulnerable, both physically and emotionally.

January 2010: The Beginning of the End

The holidays passed, and I spent a lot of time talking to the baby. I told her about our trip to North Africa in the summer of 2009. I told her of the gifts I had gotten her. I cried letting her know that I didn't have any answers, and I hoped that I was making the right decision. I told her that I hoped she would love her adoptive parents and that I knew they were kindhearted people. I introduced her to Erykah Badu and told her that she owed her life to this great musician. Sometimes when I talked to her, she'd respond with a kick or punch to my tummy.

In January I had briefly moved in with my ex due to family issues at my home. While we were living together, he continued to express his concerns about the adoption of his daughter. Despite his reservations, I knew I was making the best decision given our circumstances. We could barely afford to pay for rent with my student income and his sporadic paychecks, never mind raise a child. Reluctantly, he signed the papers that the adoption agency had been nudging him to sign since I first received a copy of the adoptive parent profiles back in September.

Meanwhile, the adoptive parents and I agreed upon potential future arrangements for postadoption visitation and contact. I requested an annual visitation and update. I envisioned picnics, holding hands with my biological daughter during visitations, an informal phone call here or there. I referred to myself as the birth mother, even while pregnant. It was in January that I would have been the perfect walking advertisement for adoption.

February 2010: Ready or Not

My due date came and went. I was horrified at the thought of a human being coming out of my vagina, so I was partly relieved.

The adoptive parents were practically my best friends as they eagerly awaited the birth of my daughter. My family was on edge as they prepared for me to go into labor any day. I wanted everyone to calm down, including myself. Still, I didn't know how much longer my back could carry the extra weight.

On February 12, after my doctor's appointment, I began to experience what felt like a failing bladder. I knew my bladder had a lot of pressure placed on it from the baby, but I didn't expect to keep peeing uncontrollably. Finally, a light bulb went off: *maybe my water broke?*

When we went to the hospital that evening, medical staff confirmed that I was leaking amniotic fluid. Apparently I was about to go into labor and I'd had no idea. The hospital staff made sure I was in a scratchy blue hospital gown and insisted that I lie down on my back despite my birth plan preference of being able to move freely. Additionally, they wanted to monitor the baby's heart rate, which would keep me connected to wires. When I asserted my preferences, the hospital staff reluctantly agreed to intermittently monitor the baby's heart rate so they could honor my wish.

After we settled into the hospital room, we played the waiting game. The medical staff warned me that if by six o'clock the next morning I was not having strong contractions, they would induce me with Pitocin because they were worried about the baby's safety. Sure enough, by six o'clock the next morning I was exhausted and there was no sign that the baby was making any progress. I was induced with Pitocin, and I was annoyed at the world for interfering with my birth experience. Everyone was in the room, and I just wanted to be alone with my baby for the last few moments.

The birth itself was very painful, both physically and emotionally. The contractions felt backbreaking, my uterus felt contorted and withering. I refused to take pain medication. By 10:40 a.m., everyone was in the room. The nurses spread my legs wide open, poking and prodding me to make sure it was really happening. I can't remember what was said or done because the pain was so intense. My mind was also malfunctioning from a lack of sleep.

At 10:43 a.m., she emerged into the world, a wrinkled baby. Her umbilical cord had been wrapped around her neck and she was purple. My heart started pounding with worry. Chaos ensued as the doctor cut the umbilical cord and took her away.

After the purple started melting away from my daughter's skin, I watched her on the heating machine from afar. The adoptive mother was cooing at her and calling her beautiful. I felt so proud of my daughter and myself for getting through the birth. I still couldn't believe that another human being had just emerged from my body. She was strong and healthy and I wanted so much to hold her.

While the adoptive mother was cradling her, the biological father announced that his family was going to come into the room, meaning that everyone else would need to leave because the room would reach maximum capacity. Tension began to rise, particularly between the adoptive mother and the biological father. Warily, the adoptive parents left the room.

During the shuffle of curious family members entering and exiting the room, I was finally able to hold my daughter. I couldn't believe how small and fragile she was. How could something so perfect come from such a flawed human being? The nurses wheeled me into the postpartum room with my daughter and the biological father followed. The nurse helped us to change her diaper and taught us how to swaddle her and I laughed nervously at how clumsy I felt at trying to be a mother for those few hours.

As I was spending time with my daughter, a nurse came in with flowers from the adoptive parents. I imagined them waiting anxiously and probably in fear that I had changed my mind, but it wasn't me they should have been worried about.

That night after my daughter was born, while we were still in the hospital, my ex-boyfriend declared that he was not going to give his daughter up for adoption. I locked myself in the bathroom and hid under the sink. He had already signed the papers needed for the adoption to continue, so no one else appeared to be worried. Despite those legal reassurances, his words devastated me. I screamed from the bathroom that I didn't want to be me. The nurses lured me out of my hiding spot, and one nurse, an adoptive mom herself, told me that I needed time alone with my daughter before making a final decision.

I never got as much time as I needed. I spent the night in the postpartum room with the adoptive parents as they cared for our daughter. My head was aching, and I cried silently so they could remain blissfully ignorant of my pain.

The next day was Valentine's Day, and my social worker wasted no time in bringing over the final adoption papers for me to sign. A part of me had grown so dark overnight, but I painted on a smile as my heart quietly broke. When the social worker and I were alone in the postpartum room together, the biological father burst in with my baby and asked me how I could give away my own daughter. He left her in my arms as I cried. The social worker looked like she was in shock. She took the baby from my arms and returned her to the adoptive parents outside the room.

Despite all the chaos, I still chose to sign the papers that day. I don't know how I did it soaked in postpartum hormones. I do believe that the presence of the adoptive parents and social worker held a power over me, and at that time I just didn't have the courage to claim my right to spend more time with my daughter before signing papers.

March 2010 to 2014: A Hidden Mother

A heavy depression stormed through me in the weeks following the adoption. It was as if an emptiness had burrowed itself into my belly, replacing the baby I once carried. I went back to work immediately so I could establish a sense of normalcy in my life. I worked at my college campus, and I remember on one particularly bad day, a fellow student with good intentions asked me how my baby was doing. I was uncertain how to respond, so I smiled and lied. My heart continued to grow darker.

I wish innocent questions from curious acquaintances had been the worst part of my heartache, but what followed was an excruciating, year-long court battle between the biological father and the adoptive parents. Most of the time I stood on the sidelines, but eventually I was dragged into the custody battle. I found myself tiptoeing around everyone's feelings and completely ignoring my need to heal. My relationship to both the adoptive parents and the biological father diminished, and I can imagine that, at times, both parties felt I had betrayed them. Regardless, the adoptive parents won the court battle and thus I was able to attempt to resume the life of a "normal college student" during my final year of college.

It took at least three years for me to come to terms with the pregnancy, the adoption, everything. Right now, I feel privileged to be able to visit with my daughter. I've been able to watch her grow through photographs and visitations. I feel blessed to witness the beautiful family my daughter is a part of, but my relationship with her parents hasn't been without its difficulties. I've found that establishing boundaries can be complicated and emotionally draining. For example, the adoptive parents did not want the birth father to e-mail them directly when communicating about the adoption. Instead, they instructed him to e-mail me, and I was to forward that communication to one of their relatives. At one point, I began to feel overwhelmed and frustrated that I was becoming the means of communication, especially so soon after the court battle. It took every bit of courage I had to let them know that I needed to heal, and I was no longer going to be the intermediary for communications.

At this juncture, my regrets are nearly nonexistent. If I could look back to the map of this journey and alter anything, it would have been to embrace my motherhood during my pregnancy instead of simply referring to myself as my daughter's birth mother. I was her only mother when I was pregnant with her and I should have respected and honored that role. Instead, I disconnected in order to prepare myself for the responsibility of safely bringing her into the world.

The role I play in my daughter's life today is ambiguous at best. Becoming a birth parent does not come with a set of guidelines. Everything feels uncertain. *Am I allowed to miss her? Am I allowed to feel guilty? Am I allowed to be happy? Am I a bad person for feeling jealous that they get to hug her every night—even if I chose for it to be that way?* I've asked myself those questions throughout the past few years. Other internal questions make me feel as if I am harboring a secret self. Biologically I am my daughter's mother, but people in my social circles aren't immediately aware of this unless I tell them. In the midst of my other roles and responsibilities, the thought of my daughter might suddenly flicker through my mind and remind me of how tightly my invisible motherhood can cling to my body. Piled beneath my to-do list and expanding obligations, I'm a hidden mother. And then the question "…but am I really a mother?" filters through my brain and cuts through my heart.

Physically, my body bears marks of motherhood. I remember when my daughter first discovered her belly button, she kept referring to it as "ba." She was curiously asking to see everyone's "ba." She turned to her mother and then her father, who both casually showed her their "ba." She laughed in bubbles, as if belly buttons were the funniest thing that could ever exist. Then she looked up to me and asked to see my "ba." My heart sank. If I showed her my "ba," the small stretch marks from my pregnancy would be revealed to all. My eyes began to water, and I had to pick myself up after that unexpected metaphorical fall. Over time I have grown to love the stretch marks her pregnancy left me, as they are clear evidence that a part of me is her mother.

When I've disclosed my hidden motherhood to others, they have either applauded my selflessness or condemned me for choosing to part with my flesh and blood. Being labeled as either a saint or sinner was initially disorienting as I began to navigate through my adoption journey, and I often felt misaligned. I would ask myself how I could concurrently be both a good and bad woman. As time has passed, it has been both scary and empowering to reject such labels and to instead embrace the messy and complicated truth of my story.

Observing my daughter discover the world has been a comforting experience despite the occasional awkward moments between the individuals involved. To watch her laugh, smile, and learn has been extremely humbling because I have realized that the bumpy ride has been completely worth it. Now every time I listen to Erykah Badu's "The Healer," I am reminded of my beautiful daughter. Near the end of the song, when Badu sings, "Say reboot, refresh, restart. Fresh page, new day..." I feel hopeful about all of the possibilities this adoption journey might lead to.

————

Angelique Miste Saavedra is a birth mother who is passionate about reproductive justice. Inspired by her own pregnancy and adoption journey, Angelique is committed to creating a world where all people with experiences across the reproductive spectrum are able to receive nonjudgmental and compassionate care. She currently volunteers as an after abortion talkline counselor and has previously volunteered as an abortion doula with the Bay Area Doula Project. She received her BA in anthropology from the University of California, Berkeley, and studied international development at the University of Oxford's Exeter College.

Story Reflection Questions

1. What is one moment in the story that stayed with you?

   _____

   _____

   _____

2. What questions did you find yourself asking as you read the story?

   _____

   _____

   _____

3. What challenged you about the story?

   _____

   _____

   _____

4. What surprised you about the story?

   _____

   _____

   _____

5. How does this story relate to your own life experience?

   _____

   _____

   _____

Harrison: Battling for the Chance to Make a Choice

Dr. Harriette E. Wimms

I was sitting on the gravely shore of the Patuxent River with a group of teenaged girls from the Catholic church my mother and I attended. The air smelled of salt and suntan lotion, and the sky above was picture-perfect blue as the gentle waves of the river lapped at the beach. It was the summer before our senior year of high school and our youth group minister, Annie, was asking us what we wanted to do with the rest of our lives. I had to make plans that would dictate "my future"—or so I had been told. Annie was twenty-two and seemed to me worldly and wise. She and I and several other members of the youth group had stolen away to the beach this day. Nestled within the confines of a mostly upper-middle class, mostly white neighborhood called Esperanza Farms, this portion of the shore was typically off-limits to all but community residents. Since one of the girls in the group lived in the community, our access to the beach was sanctioned for today.

Several of the girls talked about attending colleges I had never heard of: Vassar, Hood, Wellesley. "I'd like to study veterinary medicine," one girl mused while using a stick to write the name of her horse and then her new boyfriend in the sand.

Another girl said, "My parents want me to study business administration, but I don't know if I will."

My father and mother were both working-class folks, a retired aircraft electrician and a custodian, respectively, and we didn't talk much about colleges or future careers. As African Americans raised in the early 1900s, both of my parents experienced significant discrimination because of their racial and socioeconomic backgrounds. These experiences, instead of making them bitter, instilled in both of them a desire for continued self-improvement and the belief that education could powerfully improve personal and community circumstances. They believed that a "good education" would help me live a life easier than theirs had been. Still, their advice about my future was frequently generic, "Get good grades. Never give up. If you're going to do it, do your best. Books now, boys later. Keep up the good work." Most importantly, they let me know that they loved me immeasurably and would embrace whatever I chose to become.

Back on the beach, a few other girls talked about the "handsome and well-off" husbands they hoped to lure and catch and about the weddings they had "always dreamed of" as they flipped through *Elle* magazine. One girl said, "Oh, I want a dress kinda like this one here with the lace and the low back and a long train and flowers in my hair that match little bouquets placed throughout the church…"

There was a lull in the conversation and a few girls looked in the direction of my friend Shawna and me; we had been conspicuously quiet. I took a deep breath; I had been thinking about the future too, and I had come to a conclusion.

"Well, I don't think I'm ever getting married…"

An electric pause traveled among the girls as they stared at me. Somewhere a cricket chirped. I swallowed hard and continued, "Mostly what I want is to have a baby. That's what I really want to be, a mother. Just me and my kid, you know? Then maybe also I could become a DJ or a radio station producer or something like that…" The end of the sentence trailed off as I began to lose my nerve. The silence that followed was just a few seconds too long, and then a tittering of giggles erupted from the group,

"You are so funny! She's always saying crazy stuff like that."

I stared at them and then chuckled too. My youth group minister wasn't laughing though. Her face flushed as she responded, "You can do so much more than have babies! Go to college. Get a job. Do something so you can support yourself! You can have babies anytime. You have your whole life to do that."

————

I made that pronouncement over twenty years ago, and now I am watching my beautiful son sleep. For him, his life is a given. His existence is a certainty, as sure as the fact that the sun comes up in the morning, that we will go to the park on most sunny days after his nap, and that both of his mothers love him more than words could ever express. He is the center of our universe and he knows only that his presence brings us boundless joy (and the occasional exasperated sigh that accompanies parenting a two-year-old boy). He does not know nor will he understand for many years to come the legacy that surrounds my choices as a woman, a lesbian, and a working-class person of color, to become his birth mother.

I am one of those women who always knew, in my bones, that I was meant to be a mother. During those high school days, while my private Catholic school classmates (I attended on scholarship) talked of plans to attend college after graduation, I dreamed of strollers and baby clothes. I had also decided that I never wanted to be married to a man and considered the possibility of being a single mother. My peers and mentors scoffed at my confessions, telling me that I should focus instead on my obligation to support myself before producing offspring (as if my desire to have a child as a single woman would undoubtedly end in my reliance on public assistance). It was also suggested that as an African American woman, I should strive to achieve educational pursuits and economic advantage first, and that motherhood should be an afterthought once I became "accomplished." So I toddled off to a state university, received a degree in English, found a job in the marketing department of a publishing company, and pursued a number of unhealthy love relationships with men who "just weren't right for me."

This was before the AIDS epidemic truly hit our collective consciousness. In the early '80s, "safe sex" for me and many of my college friends meant ensuring you weren't going to become pregnant. Perhaps it was my maternal longings rising up from my subconscious, or maybe it was just stupidity, but I rarely used birth control. I know now, looking back, that I am a very lucky woman. Still there were many times when I would look at the calendar, feeling a dull ache in my breasts and faint nausea in the pit of my stomach, and anxiously add up the days and wonder if I had made a choice by default. Sometimes weeks would pass, and then finally my period would arrive, and I would feel I had dodged and simultaneously been struck by a bullet: relieved and saddened that my choice to become a mother had not been made for me by my contraceptive choices.

In 1992 I married one of those "not good for me" men, and after a tumultuous and abusive year of matrimonial discord and unprotected sex, I still was not pregnant. The medical establishment and women's magazines told me that this failure to conceive was cause for concern. For a woman under thirty-five, a year of sex without pregnancy suggested that there was a problem. For a woman thirty-five or over, six months was the time frame for panic. I had, in fact, married my husband with the intention of having children—the marriage itself was an afterthought. And somehow, between our fights and his drinking, between the money problems and the lies, I had managed to chart my basal body temperature religiously for months and was having sex at all of the fertilely appropriate times. My gynecologist agreed that I might have some "reproductive challenges" and sent me to a specialist.

I was diagnosed with an endocrine disorder called polycystic ovarian syndrome (a disorder that meant I did not ovulate regularly), as well as a severe case of hypothyroidism and a hearty case of depression. An endocrinologist and a fertility specialist whom I soon consulted were eager to help me become pregnant. They talked cheerily about the medications and procedures (from artificial insemination to in vitro fertilization) that could help me and urged me to move forward as soon as I was able.

"There's much we can try—from oral medications to induce ovulation to more high-tech methods to help you achieve pregnancy. As your doctor, I can't make your life decisions for you. But given your health problems, you might want to move forward on starting your family within the next several months. You've been married almost a year now, right? So it's about time to get started. And luckily, most employers in Maryland are now required to include fertility treatment coverage in their health insurance benefits packages." She rifled through my file and continued, "We do accept your insurance. So your treatments will be covered at ninety percent of the allowed benefit. We'll start with Clomid and some fertility monitoring, which should run you about fifty dollars per cycle. If that sounds doable, we should be able to move forward as soon as you're ready. Perhaps your husband will be able to make it to the next visit?"

While my doctors were enthusiastic about me getting pregnant, my husband was not as enthused. He refused to attend appointments with me and was not very thrilled about the prospect of his fertility screening: he was more comfortable to shrug off our childlessness as my problem and to leave it at that. Still my specialists were hopeful. The doctors, nurses, and insurance representatives all seemed to believe that our "right" to procreate was a given, despite the ongoing havoc within our home.

My husband and I were on the outs for a number of reasons, the least of which being that I had fallen in love with a woman. As my marriage disintegrated in 1993, my divorce was accompanied by a sense of relief and freedom. I had a job writing marketing copy and filing paperwork for a publishing company with good benefits and room for advancement. I had a nice enough place to live: a rambling, drafty three-story Victorian I rented with three friends in a sketchy but culturally and racially diverse community in Baltimore City. I was finally living an authentic life: I joined book clubs, kissed women in bars, volunteered at the lesbian bookstore, coedited a literary magazine, sat in cafes reading poetry, placed a rainbow sticker on the bumper of my car, attended coming-out support groups at the local gay community center— and I was still mightily determined to become pregnant. In 1996 I met my future partner, Pat, who answered my personal ad in the city paper.

During our first conversation, while we flirted and talked about music we enjoyed and vacation spots we hoped to visit one day, I interrupted her to say, "You know, I like you and I want to get to know you better and everything. But in all honesty, I have to tell you upfront that I'm planning to get pregnant next year, whether or not I am in a relationship. If you don't like kids, we probably should hang up now."

There was a moment of silence on the phone, and then I could hear the smile in her voice as she said, "I'm still on the phone, aren't I? So, want to have dinner tomorrow night?"

We fell in love and, in typical lesbian fashion, we rented a moving van three months later. My parents fell in love with her; my nieces and nephews were awed by her video game and comic book collection. We planned a commitment ceremony in fall 1997; when we returned from our honeymoon, we called the fertility doctor's office to make an appointment. Motherhood, as the doctors had told me five years prior, was probably only a few prescriptions and a syringe or two away. Unfortunately, I didn't understand that the reproductive rules had changed drastically with my marital status.

Now that I was divorced, I was considered a single woman by fertility specialists and my insurance company, whether or not I was involved in a same-sex relationship. I learned of these changes when I went to the appointment with my reproductive endocrinologist. Once so enthusiastic, her demeanor was somber as I entered her office.

"Well, now that you're divorced, things are a bit different," she said. "You need to call your insurance company first and find out if your treatments will be covered. Unfortunately, many of my single clients have a hard time getting these kinds of procedures covered."

"But I'm not single. Plus, I'm infertile."

"In the eyes of the law you are single," she said. Her jaw was set, almost defensive. She sat up straight in her chair.

"This is just how the regulations are written. Insurance companies usually only cover fertility treatments for heterosexual married couples. But you can always pay out of pocket and see if they'll reimburse you."

I can recall that I just couldn't understand the words she was saying. They just did not compute. It couldn't possibly be true that insurance companies could discriminate on the basis of marital status, could it? Surely that had to be illegal. This, however, was just the beginning. I learned from talking to medical office support staff, the Maryland Office of the attorney general, and the benefits coordinator at my job, that this was in fact how my policy (and most policies) was written. The policies were blatantly discriminatory but legally so.

Therefore, despite my diagnosis of medical conditions that cause infertility, fertility treatments were not covered because of my sexual orientation. Motherhood was no longer the medical necessity it had been when I was a heterosexual married woman. Procedures that might have cost me fifty or one hundred dollars out of pocket while I was married to a man would now cost me several thousand dollars per month. I was afraid I would be denied the opportunity to become a mother because I could not afford the medical procedures I needed and had once been offered so easily when I was married to a man.

I contacted our local ACLU office to find out if what was happening was legal. The representative I spoke with said I was not the first woman to relay this kind of story. The lawyer believed I had a case, but if I chose to pursue it I might draw significant media coverage. I declined their help, afraid that my job would be jeopardized by the negative press.

I began writing letters: to the human resources department of my employer, to the appeals department of my insurance company, to the Maryland insurance commissioner, and to the office of the attorney general, encouraging them to change their policies. But in the end, I was told nothing could be done.

What's worse, many physicians seemed to believe that my desire to become a mother was no longer a right or even a reasonable consideration. My fertility specialist suggested to me, over the phone, that I find a different practitioner because my insurance would not cover her services. Several hospitals and fertility treatment centers outright refused to provide me services because I was a lesbian, above and beyond any ability to pay.

One day I even walked into the office of a reproductive endocrinologist in the same professional building as my dentist. A picture of a mother and child on the door had caught my attention and I thought, *Maybe this is a sign.* The office was wallpapered in muted pink-and-blue swirls with faded silk flower arrangements on several end tables. The waiting room was empty.

A receptionist pushed back a glass window. "Ye-ess. May I help you?"

"Yes," I said. "I have a quick question: Does the doctor offer services to single women or lesbians?"

She said hesitantly, "You'll have to talk with the doctor about that."

"Well, is the doctor available? I'm having a hard time finding a doctor who will work with me, and I'd like to talk to him to ask…"

"No, hon," she interrupted. "The doctor isn't available. He only sees people by appointment."

"What about a nurse or the office manager?" I replied in nearly a whisper.

"No, ma'am. You'll have to ask the doctor about that."

I left the office after grabbing the doctor's card. That afternoon the same receptionist transferred my call immediately to the physician. I asked him about his willingness to offer artificial insemination to lesbian couples.

"I can't help you," he said.

"I'm sorry?"

"No, I cannot help you. I don't approve of that sort of thing." And he hung up the phone.

The next week I called the department of reproductive medicine at one of the most prestigious hospitals and universities in Maryland. When told that I could not access fertility services there, I asked to speak to the head of the department. The doctor returned my call late one afternoon. "How may I help you?" he asked.

I told him that I had been diagnosed with PCOS and had not become pregnant after nearly two years of unprotected sex with my former husband. And then I told him about my domestic partnership and how many doctors I had contacted would not offer artificial insemination services to us.

"Miss Wimms," he said. "We simply can't offer those services to you because you are not married. This is of course not a value judgment. You must look at it from the hospital's standpoint. If we inseminate you and then let's say you die, the hospital would be liable."

"I don't understand," I said, perplexed.

"We could be sued for paternity."

I laughed out loud before I could catch myself and realize he was serious.

"Well," I said, recovering, "what if I sign some kind of contract that states you won't be sued if I die?"

"Our lawyers wouldn't allow us to do that. Good day."

Crying in my internist's office a few months later, I relayed these stories while discussing which depression medication we should try next. The doctor pulled out a notepad and wrote down a name and number. "Call this woman. She's young and has just joined a practice in this neighborhood. She might help you."

Pat and I went to the appointment together. As we stepped into the doctor's office, I felt as though I were walking into battle. After shaking her hand, we sat down in the overstuffed chairs in front of the desk. She moved to the leather chair behind the desk and sat down, smiling.

"We are a lesbian couple," I said.

I looked up and she was still smiling.

"Great," she said. "How can I help you?"

Once my partner and I finally had located a doctor who was willing to help us get pregnant, she told us that Maryland law stipulated that an "unmarried" woman could only be inseminated in a doctor's office using sperm that had been frozen, stored, and quarantined for six months at a cryobank. This would cost several hundred dollars. If we were using anonymous donor sperm, we could move forward. But if we wanted our child to have a relationship with his or her donor, we would have to have sperm processed. Pat and I had decided that we wanted our child to have the option of knowing his donor. We asked a dear friend to be our donor and he agreed. So we chose a sperm bank that had served lesbians for years and made preparations to have our donor visit the bank.

However, as the appointment date approached, the bank called to notify us that our known donor would not be able to provide sperm specimens for us if he was gay. It was the policy of the bank to disallow anonymous donors who were gay due to an "increased risk of HIV disease." This rule extended to known donors as well. Therefore, we had now lost our ability to choose a known donor for our child.

While my partner and I struggled to deal with the many physical and emotional challenges associated with my disorder, we simultaneously were struggling to address and combat our many confusing bureaucratic problems.

Then one day our gynecologist announced to us that she was pregnant and moving to Colorado. After three years of fighting this system, with this news of our doctor's pregnancy, my partner and I decided to give up. We were tired. A choice had been made for us, borne out of our frustration and inability to access the technology to support our reproductive choices. We had networked with many women who were making the choice to become parents as single women or lesbian couples, but it seemed that the rules were different for infertile lesbian couples.

Still, after several conversations with the cryobank director, she made the decision to allow gay known donors. After countless conversations with human resources for the university and hospital that had denied us access to fertility services, the medical institution has now become a leader in helping lesbian couples in Baltimore conceive, and the university offers employee insurance benefits that cover fertility treatments for lesbian couples.

Two years later, I was talking to my friend Leslie about my "choice" not to have children. Leslie had shared an office with me at my first job out of college and we had become very close because of it. She had witnessed my fertility struggles from the beginning of my first marriage. I told her, "I've decided to go back to school. I'm thinking about getting a graduate degree in child psychology. That way I can still help and support children even if I never have my own."

"Umm-hmm," Leslie said.

"And I figure a PhD is going to cost me about what it would have cost to get pregnant anyway," I chuckled.

She didn't laugh.

I believed I would eventually embrace a "child-free" life with my partner. Perhaps we would come to enjoy being able to travel at the drop of a hat, to have quiet dinners and romantic late-night talks, and to live our lives with each other.

"And one day," I said tentatively, "maybe one day I will be able to adopt when my heart is open...and when I can find an agency that will work with gay couples."

"You know, I just don't buy this," Leslie responded.

"What?"

"This whole child-free business. You've always wanted to have children. Yes, it has been really hard, and I can't believe that the cards have been so stacked against you. But this is not the Harriette I know. You usually fight harder when faced with a challenge. I just don't believe this is the end of this story."

Her statement spurred me to action. Surely there had to be individuals who were willing to help us achieve reproductive equity, and I became determined to find them. I had joined a listserv for lesbian moms in 1995. Sitting at work, I had typed the terms, "lesbian" and "mother" into a search engine and up popped a link for the "lesbian moms list." The listserv was composed of a few hundred women from around the world who were lesbian or bisexual mothers. These women had children conceived or adopted during previous heterosexual relationships or within same-sex relationships. The list also included women hoping and planning to become lesbian mothers.

I now began telling these women about our struggles and inquiring about other online supports and advocacy agencies. Through this list-serv I also found online support groups for women with PCOS who were trying to conceive, for infertile lesbians, and for overweight women who were trying to conceive. We all shared tactics for finding open-minded practitioners, strategies for handling the stressors involved in dealing with infertility and discrimination, as well as methods for boosting fertility and riding the rollercoaster of infertility treatments.

The women on these lists became cheerleaders when I was feeling downhearted, fitness and health partners, legal advocates when I needed help to bolster my argument with a benefits coordinator or insurance company representative, and comrades when I needed someone to share in my righteous anger. These women helped me believe again that my dream of motherhood was as much my right as a lesbian as it had been when I was married to a man. Through these networks I eventually put together a new team of doctors to aggressively treat my medical conditions and who supported Pat and me in our desire to have a child. We were also referred to a local cryobank willing to process sperm specimens from our known donor with no question about his sexual orientation (we processed enough sperm for eleven months of attempts, which cost about $4500). Through these grassroots support networks, we also found an insurance loophole that meant each monthly cycle of fertility treatments cost us $850 rather than $5000.

In June of 2003, we joyfully began trying to conceive our child. The first month was so exciting: Pat and I driving together to pick up our "swimmers" from the sperm bank and delivering them to the fertility center (with a sign taped to the car window that read "Baby on Board"). But despite a combination of oral fertility medication, fertility monitoring including ultrasounds and ovulation predictor kits, and perfectly timed inseminations, we could not become pregnant. After our fifth failed attempt, our fertility specialist called. She was concerned that the oral medication we were using was not strong enough and that our next step was to move to fertility medication by injection. Each month of medication would cost between $600 and $1200, in addition to the insemination costs. Our credit cards were now nearly maxed out with fertility treatment costs, and we just didn't know where we would find the money or the emotional resolve to move on to the "injectable cycles." We definitely would not be able to afford IVF (at $12,000 per month not including medication) because my insurance company would not cover any of the costs. We simply couldn't afford to get pregnant.

We opted to try one more month of the less-expensive oral medication, and then we would call it quits. Eight days after that insemination, I started vomiting and my breasts were so sore I could barely place my arms at my sides. At twelve days past that insemination, blood work confirmed that I was indeed pregnant. And two weeks later, on the black-and-white ultrasound screen, we saw the tiny beating heart of our baby. Ten years in the making, our son's heart had begun its lifelong rhythm.

I have been, and always will be, pro-choice. Since that moment when my partner and I watched our son's flickering heartbeat, I've struggled with my pro-choice stance. I maintain that I am pro-choice, but antiabortion and opposed to abortion as a method of birth control...but I apply these beliefs to myself only. After the experiences my partner and I have had, when outside forces dictated if and how we would conceive our child, we know the necessity of providing access to choices.

My mother, who passed away in October 2006 at the age of eighty-three, was a devout Catholic. Despite her strong belief in the church's doctrine, she would tell anyone who would listen that church and state have no business messing around with a woman's body and her right to choose. This from a woman who had birthed seven children, whose children had provided her with twenty grandchildren, twenty-nine great-grandchildren, and one great-great-grandchild.

My son was delivered via planned C-section at thirty-eight weeks gestational age after months of weekly ultrasounds and nonstress tests, as well as a short stint of bed rest. Although I had dreamed of him for so long, fought for him for so long, nothing could have prepared me for how much we would fall in love with Harrison from the moment we laid eyes on him. When I looked at him for the first time, I realized that my longing when I was a naïve sixteen-year-old was for him. I was not only meant to be a mother, I was meant to be *his* mother. I am so grateful to have been granted the constellations of blessings and hard work that led him to us.

Harrison is thriving. He loves to play in mud puddles and run as fast as he can down grass-covered hills. He has temper tantrums and loves to scream at the top of his lungs from time to time for no good reason. He is always well dressed, well fed, has more books than any child I know, and knows implicitly that he is loved by me (his mommy), by Pat (his momma), by our donor (his uncle Jason), and by a host of our friends who make up his incredible chosen family.

But our story does not end there.

Our lives felt like a fairy-tale in those first few weeks. Yes, we were exhausted (during the first week of Harrison's life, Pat was so exhausted that she would fall asleep and snore for just a moment each time she blinked). But we had become the family of our dreams. We settled into an ongoing cycle of nursing, diaper changes, nuzzling, and sleep. I returned to work five weeks after my son was born because, as a graduate student, that was all the maternity leave available to me. Pat remained at home to care for our son.

When I began falling asleep at work or behind the wheel of my car and experiencing tingling on one side of my face and trouble speaking, my internist thought I was having strange postpartum symptoms. When my hearing started to disappear, a CAT scan identified two tumors, one in my ear and another in the frontal cortex of my brain, which were responsible for my symptoms. Two weeks later, when my son was just four months old, neurosurgeons removed a large meningioma from within the left side of my skull. Six months later, a second tumor was removed from my inner ear, leaving me deaf in my left ear.

Pat adopted Harrison as his "second parent" when he was ten months old. After reading the glowing letters written by our friends in support of our family, the judge happily deemed Pat a "legally fit and proper" parent for Harrison. I burst into tears in the courtroom. We fell into a comfortable rhythm of daily life, all our affairs circling day and night around our precious Harrison; however, the orbit between Pat and me became ever wider.

Perhaps it was the stressors involved in caring for a new baby while dealing with multiple health challenges, or maybe it was my struggle to simultaneously work toward the completion of my PhD while parenting an infant, or maybe it was the sleep deprivation and the fact that my partner and I stopped having sex after our son was born, or maybe it was all the years of battling against outside foes that had led us to finally turn on each other in their absence. But for whatever the reasons, these events eventually led us to end our ten-year marriage the month following my mother's death.

My ex-wife and I are working hard to remain the best parenting partners we can be to Harrison. We have made the choice, for now, to live separate lives as well as support our son and perhaps rekindle the friendship and mutual support that helped us create him in the first place. In many ways that premonition of single motherhood from so long ago has eerily come to pass.

I'd thought that if I did become pregnant that our child should have a sibling by birth or adoption. But at age thirty-nine, with a complicated medical history, adoption is a challenge for me: I would face difficulty passing the physical screening many adoption agencies require. My physical health also prohibits me from becoming pregnant again. Moreover, the costs of medical and fertility treatments have not left me enough money for the costs involved in adoption.

For today, the sun is shining, my son is stirring from his nap, and the playground is calling. For today, my choice to be his mother means embracing with gratitude the miracle that is Harrison: a child born triumphantly out of a battle for choice. And for today, at least, this is enough.

———

Dr. Harriette E. Wimms is the Child and Adolescent Behavioral Health Program Development and Clinical Manager at Chase Brexton Health Centers, an LGBTQ friendly Federally Qualified Health Center in Baltimore, Maryland. Her expertise spans from supporting families who have children with disabilities to providing interventions and professional development seminars. Dr. Wimms holds a PhD in psychology from the University of Maryland, Baltimore County, and has received specialty training in the areas of child clinical psychology and community and social psychology. She also holds a master's degree in developmental psychology from Johns Hopkins University and a bachelor's degree in English from Towson State University. Dr. Wimms has served as the director of inpatient pediatric psychology services at Mt. Washington Pediatric Hospital and serves on the boards of several organizations supporting marginalized citizens. Most importantly, Harriette is honored to be the proud and lucky mother of her son, Harrison, age ten and absolutely amazing and brilliant (in her humble opinion).

Story Reflection Questions

1. What is one moment in the story that stayed with you?

    _____

    _____

    _____

2. What questions did you find yourself asking as you read the story?

    _____

    _____

    _____

3. What challenged you about the story?

    _____

    _____

    _____

4. What surprised you about the story?

    _____

    _____

    _____

5. How does this story relate to your own life experience?

    _____

    _____

    _____

If

Susan Ito

We had been married just less than a year in that spring of 1989. My husband had a medical conference in Washington. He left our home in California early in the week, and I planned to meet him there later for a long weekend. When the airport van arrived at our house, I loaded my suitcase into the back, strapped myself in, and fell asleep before we reached the bottom of our street. The driver shook me awake at the airport; I had been drooling on my jacket collar. I had never experienced such overwhelming somnolence before. I stumbled through the corridors of the airport, feeling drugged, my head buzzing with a strange, sparkling heaviness. All I wanted to do was curl into a corner and sleep, the passengers rushing past me with their wheeled luggage, their tickets flapping in their hands. It was all I could do to stagger onto the plane and doze, waking only to devour the plastic tray of rubbery food and sleep again.

"I think I'm sick," I told John as I got off the plane. "I feel woozy."

But it had been the first month of sex without birth control, the little cervical cap far, far away in the bathroom cabinet, the spermicide buried in the underwear drawer. We had thought it would take months, maybe even a year. Not so soon as this.

I sat on the edge of the bed and flipped through the phone book, searching for a clinic that would be open on a Saturday. While John was in a darkened auditorium, studying the dark red planet of a diseased liver shining huge and luminous on the wall, I climbed into a taxi,

---

trembling, and gave the driver the address of the Georgetown Women's Center.

They took a tube full of blood from my arm and then told me to call back in three hours. I wandered the streets of a city I didn't know, the jeweled boutiques, bookstores, a café with colorful bowls of salad crowded together under a glass counter. I sat there, eating stuffed grape leaves, staring at my watch, the tiny needle of the second hand jerking through space.

I thought about my blood, the tablespoons of blood that lay in the glass tube in the clinic. Blood that was waiting to speak, its language translated by chemicals and microscopes. Blood of the birth mother I'd tracked down and met when I was twenty, who had been glad to know me but wanted me to stay a lifelong secret. Blood of my invisible birth father, whose name she wouldn't reveal to me. Blood of so many unknown relatives. This blood was going to inform me of the presence of another, of one whose face I would finally see, a child to name and hold.

The woman on the phone said yes. "Congratulations," she said—news that she delivered dozens of times a day, altering lives with one syllable. Yes. No. I stared at the plastic receiver, the telephone. The phone was bolted to a wall outside of a B. Dalton bookstore. I bought a book on pregnancy and ran my finger along the due-date chart, counting months. Early January. New year, new life.

———

I remember almost nothing about that pregnancy except the way that it ended. I remember a walk along the grassy trails of Sea Ranch, the wild wind, my bursting energy. I was wearing John's blue jeans to accommodate my five-month-pregnant belly.

In August, we took a trip to the Outer Banks in North Carolina with his brother's family. I swelled in the humidity like a sponge, my breasts enormous, my face squishy with fluid. "Look at me," I said, frowning in the mirror.

"You look wonderful," he said.

It wasn't what I was talking about. I hadn't been complaining about feeling fat or unattractive, although I *was* fat, in a strange, swollen way.

John, a doctor, went from that family vacation to El Salvador, heading a medical delegation to the war zone of Guazapa, under the volcano. My father-in-law disapproved, told me outright that he felt John was abandoning me. But I was proud of the work we were involved in. While he was in Central America, I drove to Davis to help load a container of wheelchairs, crutches, and medicine bound for Nicaragua. It was then that I noticed I couldn't lace my sneakers. My feet were the size of small footballs.

I picked him up at the airport, saying, "Don't you think I look fat?"

"You're pregnant, sweetheart," he said. "That's how you're supposed to look."

Sunday morning. September 17, 1989. I had gained thirteen pounds in a week. I pulled out the pregnancy book. In red print, it said, *Call the doctor if you gain more than three pounds in one week. If your face or hands or feet are swollen.* If. If. If. I checked them all off. While John was in the shower, I called my obstetrician and friend, Lisa. I whispered under the sound of running water, "I think something is wrong."

Lisa's voice was so smooth, so calm. "Swelling is very common," she said, "but it would be a good idea to get a blood pressure check. Can John do it?"

We stopped by his office, two blocks from the restaurant we had decided on for dinner. We were going to see a movie, then browse a bookstore; our usual date. I hopped onto the exam table, held out my arm. I couldn't wait to get to la Méditerranée. My mouth had been dreaming of spanakopita all day.

I heard the Velcro tearing open on the cuff, felt its smooth blue band wrapping around me. I swung my feet and smiled up at John, the stethoscope around his neck, loved this small gesture of taking care of me. I felt the cuff tightening, the pounding of my heart echoing up and down my fingers and through my elbow.

The expression on his face I will never forget, the change in color from pink to ash, as if he had died standing at my side. "Lie down," he said quietly. "Lie down on your left side. *Now.*"

The numbers were all wrong, two hundred plus, over and over again, his eyes darkening as he watched the mercury climb on the wall. He shook his head. "What's Lisa's phone number?"

His voice was grim as he spoke to her on the phone—numbers, questions, a terrible urgency. He told me to go into the tiny bathroom and pee into a cup. "We've got to dipstick your urine, see if there's any protein."

I sat on the toilet and listened to him crash through the cupboards, knocking over samples of ulcer pills, brochures about stomach cancer, looking for a container of thin paper tabs. I gave him the paper cup, the gold liquid cloudy and dense. The dipstick changed color quickly, from white to powdery blue to sky to deep indigo. My protein level was off the chart. "No," he whispered. "No, no, goddamn it, no."

I asked what, over and over, not believing that things could be as bad as what his face was telling me. "Your kidneys aren't working," he said. He pulled me out the door, across the street to the hospital. He pounded the buttons of the elevator, pulled me flying to the nurses' station, spat numbers at them. I thought, *Don't be a bully; nurses hate doctors who are bullies*, but they scattered like quail, one of them on the phone, another pushing me, stumbling, into a room. There were three of them pulling at my clothes, my shoes; the blood pressure cuff again; the shades were drawn; they moved so swiftly, with such seriousness.

I had a new doctor now. Lisa, obstetrician of the normal, was instantly off my case, and I was assigned a special neonatologist named Weiss. He was perfectly bald, with thick glasses and wooden clogs, a soft voice.

A squirt of blue gel on my belly for the fetal monitor, the galloping sound of hoofbeats, the baby riding a wild pony inside me. What a relief to hear that sound, although I didn't need the monitor; I could feel the baby punching at my liver.

There was a name for what I had. Preeclampsia. Ah. Well, preeclampsia was certainly better than eclampsia, and as long as it was pre, then they could stop it, couldn't they? And what was eclampsia? An explosion of blood pressure, a flood of protein poisoning the blood, kidney failure, the vessels in spasm, a stroke, seizures, blindness, death. But I didn't have any of those things. I had *pre*eclampsia. It felt safe.

They slipped a needle into my wrist, hung a bag of magnesium sulfate. "This is to prevent seizures," they said. "You may feel a little hot."

As the first drops of the drug slipped into my bloodstream, I felt a flash of electricity inside my mouth. My tongue was baking. My scalp prickled, burning, and I threw up onto the sheets. I felt as if I was being microwaved.

I was wheeled down to radiology. Pictures of the baby onscreen, waving, treading water. A real child, not a pony or a fish. The X-ray tech, a woman with curly brown hair and a red Coca-Cola T-shirt, asked, "Do you want to know the sex?" I sat up. "There you go." She pointed. A flash between the legs, like a finger. A boy. I nearly leapt off the gurney. "John! Did you see? A boy! It's Samuel!" Sahm-*well*, the Spanish pronunciation, named after our surrogate father in Nicaragua, the most dignified man we knew.

He didn't want to look, couldn't celebrate having a son. He knew so much more than I did.

———

Weiss came to stand next to my bed. Recited numbers slowly.

"Baby needs at least two more weeks for viability. He's already too small, way too small. But you..." He looked at me sadly, shook his head. "You probably can't survive two weeks without having a stroke, seizures, worse." He meant I could die.

"What are the chances...that we could both make it?" Doctors are always talking percentages.

"Less than ten percent, maybe less than five percent." The space between his fingers shrunk into nothing.

This is how they said it. I was toxemic, poisoned by pregnancy. My only cure was to not be pregnant anymore. The baby needed two more weeks, just fourteen days.

I looked at John hopefully. "I can wait. It will be all right."

"Honey. Your blood pressure is through the roof. Your kidneys are shutting down. You are *on the verge of having a stroke.*"

I actually smiled at him. I actually said that having a stroke at twenty-nine would not be a big deal. I was a physical therapist; I knew about rehab. I could rehabilitate myself. I could walk with a cane. Lots of people do it. I had a bizarre image of leaning on the baby's carriage, supporting myself the way elderly people use a walker.

We struggled through the night. "I'm not going to lose this baby," I said.

"I'm not going to lose *you*," he said. "And think of the baby. Chances are almost certain that a baby born this small will have problems. Severe problems."

I knew about children with problems; I had worked in a children's cerebral palsy clinic for years. Many of them had been born at the same gestational age as Samuel was now. I knew children who could not walk or speak or look into their mother's eyes.

After the longest night of my life, I relented.

I lay with my hands on my belly all night, feeling Samuelito's limbs turning this way and that. There was nothing inside me that could even think of saying good-bye.

———

At four in the morning, I called my parents. "We're in trouble," I said. My mother wept, frantic, alone. "I've got to find Daddy." He was on the road, traveling somewhere—where? North Carolina, Kentucky, Tennessee? On the road meant invisible, unreachable, gone. "I'll come out there tomorrow," she said. "There's no reason," I told her. She hung up sobbing.

At six o'clock, I called my birth mother. She was calm, optimistic, her voice smooth as water. "I've known women who've had the same thing, and everything always turns out fine."

"It won't be fine; it's too early, way too early..." I wanted to tell her I wasn't *like* the others she'd known, that 95 percent of preeclampsia cases happen when the baby is nearly full term.

She wasn't listening. "I'm sure everything will be *fine*." Her voice was flat, gentle. She didn't offer to fly out to California. I wondered about the stroke, if it really happened, if that would bring her to my bedside. I began to get a small glimmering inside me, of understanding what it means to be a parent. And seeing for the first time that this was what she was not.

———

I had met her when I was twenty, after a heart-racing, detective-story search. She was beautiful, glamorous, sophisticated: I felt I had hit the birth-mother jackpot. Over the years it became clear that she was willing to be my friend and confidante, that she liked me. But there were two key conditions I had to adhere to if I wanted a relationship with her: One, I had to keep my own identity a secret in front of anyone she knew; and two, I had to not ask her who my birth father was. At the time, it seemed worth it. I was young and infatuated by her charisma; I was willing to agree to anything. She also charmed my parents, who had fully supported my searching for her.

———

September 18, 1989. Another day of magnesium sulfate, the cuff that inflated every five minutes, the fetal monitor booming through the room. No change in status for either of us.

I signed papers of consent, my hand moving numbly across the paper, my mind screaming, *I do* not *consent, I do* not, *I do not.*

In the evening, Weiss's associate entered with a tray, a syringe, and a nurse with mournful eyes.

"It's just going to be a bee sting," he said.

And it was, a small tingle, quick pricking bubbles under my navel, and then a thing like a tiny drinking straw that went in and out with a barely audible pop. It was so fast. I thought, *I love you, I love you, you must be hearing this, please hear me.* And then a Band-Aid was unwrapped, with its plastic smell of childhood, and spread onto my belly.

"All done," he said. All done.

My child was inside swallowing the fizzy drink, and it bubbled against his tiny tongue like a bud, the deadly soda pop.

This is what it was. A drug, injected into my womb, a drug to stop his heart. To lay him down to sleep, so he wouldn't feel what would happen the next day, the terrible, terrible thing that would happen. *Evacuation* is what it is called in medical journals.

Evacuees are what the Japanese Americans were called when they were ripped from their homes, tagged like animals, flung into the desert. Evacuated, exiled, thrown away.

I lay on my side pinching the pillowcase. I wondered if he would be startled by the drug's taste, if it was bitter, or strange, or just different from the salt water he was used to. I prayed that it wouldn't be noxious, not like the magnesium sulfate, that it wouldn't hurt. That it would be fast.

John sat next to the bed and held one hand as I pressed the other against my belly. I looked over his shoulder into the dark slice of night between the heavy curtains. Samuel, Samuelito, jumped against my hand once. He leaped through the space into the darkness and then was gone.

All gone.

———

This was my first experience of being a mother. I went home at the end of the week, gushing fluid, peeing and sweating quarts of the liquids my body hadn't been able to release. I wept oceans.

My parents called me several times a day. "Is there anything you need? What can we do for you?" I could imagine them wringing their hands, pacing, feeling helpless.

"Nothing," I said dully. *I need my baby.*

———

It was a week before I called my birth mother again. Her voice was bright.

"Oh!" she said, surprised. "When I didn't hear back from you again, I assumed everything must have turned out all right." Seven days, I thought, seven days and she never called.

"It didn't turn out all right," I said, my voice as dull and heavy as a stone. First grandchild swept away and she never picked up the phone.

"Well," she said (how could her voice be so calm?), "I'm very sorry. You're so young though…"

Is that what she told herself, at twenty-nine, when she had me and then let me go? Did she just set her vision to the future, the other children she would have? Was it really that easy?

There weren't many choices for my birth mother when she was pregnant with me back then. It's possible that she could have taken a knitting needle or rat poison and tried to terminate the pregnancy herself; I'm thankful, for both her sake and mine that she didn't do that. She might have run away to an anonymous town where nobody knew her and passed herself off as a widow with a child. But that would have meant tearing herself away from her family, her community, and everything she knew.

So she did what felt like the only viable option at the time: She bought a girdle. She ate like a bird. She did what she could do to ensure that I would be as small as possible; then she traveled to a faraway city and gave birth to me two months prematurely.

And then she gave me up for adoption.

Her choices had begun narrowing long before that day, however. They started shrinking when, in 1941, our country went to war with Japan, whose people looked like her family. Her family had no choice when their Los Angeles business was shut down and they were told to pack their lives into a single trunk, and they were forced to show their allegiance by moving into a barbed-wire compound in the high dusty desert of Colorado. She was ten years old then.

They had little option when the war ended and they were offered sponsorship, a job, a home, and a place in a tiny town in the Midwest. Everyone in this town originated, one generation or two or three, from the same small country in Europe. Her family would become a charitable, benevolent experiment: loved but untouchable. When she reached adulthood, it was expected that she would choose a solitary life, the life of a schoolteacher or a nurse. The life of a wife did not seem an option because who in that community could openly marry such an outsider?

She chose love, a secret love. She chose a married man with a family. And that was how I came to be.

———

When I was twenty-five, and in a fragile, new relationship, I felt myself experiencing strange sensations: swollen, hypersensitive breasts and the impulse to weep every five minutes. It took a while for me to understand what might be happening.

I picked up the telephone book, scanned the millions of numbers, flipping the thin yellow pages, and dialed. *Crisis Pregnancy Center.* I certainly felt like I was experiencing a crisis. I spoke with a woman who told me to come that day. I pressed the white buttons on the phone and called my boyfriend. My mouth was dry as I told him where I was going. He had only the year before gone through a pregnancy with another girlfriend; he had seen her through the entire thing, held her hand through labor and birth, and together they had signed relinquishment papers for their daughter's adoption. He didn't say much when I told him what I feared; he was in shock.

He drove me to a place in the outer Richmond district, by the beach, a small white door in the basement of a church. A woman in a plain brown dress opened it, scouring us both with her eyes. "Did you call this morning?" I nodded and handed over a brown paper bag that held a mayonnaise jar, sloshing with warm urine. She told us to wait in what looked like a daycare room, with blue and yellow padded mats on the floor and a plastic playhouse littered with stuffed animals. We sat on short chairs, our knees tilted up to the ceiling. Thirty minutes later, the woman called us into a windowless room, sat us down on a worn loveseat, and said that I was pregnant.

The world became very quiet. I believed that I could hear the little ball of cells popping and dividing underneath my skin. I imagined a tiny seahorse rocking in a crimson pear. The woman began talking about baby clothes and financial assistance for unwed mothers and then paused and squinted at me. "You aren't considering abortion, are you?"

I couldn't lift my eyes. "I don't know."

"Well. Let me tell you about what *really* goes on in that procedure." Her lips curled away from her teeth. "What happens is this. Your baby is sucked out of your body by a machine that is *fifteen times more powerful* than your household vacuum cleaner! Can you imagine?"

I told her that I couldn't imagine. Then I stood up to leave, telling her I would think about it. My boyfriend's face was gray as stone. He reached out to take my hand.

The woman moved to the door, blocking us a bit. Taking slow long looks at each of us, she warned, "You might want to consider the fact that the majority of relationships deteriorate after an abortion." We thanked her and walked to the ocean.

Pregnant. It couldn't be possible. I clutched at the front of my jeans, stumbling in the sand. "I'm scared," I said. Tears ran down into the collar of my shirt. And then, "No wonder I'm crying all the time."

He squinted out at the ocean, his eyes bright. I knew what he was thinking. *Not again. Not again.*

It seemed that there were three possible options: abortion, adoption, or keeping the baby ourselves. Adoption was out of the question: there was no way I was going to relinquish my first blood relative, and there was no way he was going to endure that particular hell again. Keeping the baby, at that point in our lives, seemed as abstract and unrealistic as becoming astronauts or movie stars. Our relationship was too new, and we were way too unequipped. My parents were extraordinarily conservative and old-fashioned, and I couldn't imagine even admitting to them that I had had sex. Some people might, at the age of twenty-five, decide to up and raise a baby with a person they barely knew. But it seemed absolutely incomprehensible to me.

Abortion felt like the only avenue.

I was fascinated though—horrified and fascinated—to realize that my body was capable of doing such a thing. Growing a human being. I patted the skin over my belly, trying to feel something, although it was ludicrous; surely it was no larger than a paper clip. I knew that its days were numbered, and I resolved not to miss any part of it, to feel everything I could until it was gone.

***

I called her. There was no question of calling my parents. I called my birth mother because I knew she would understand. And of course she did. She had been an alarmed, unmarried pregnant girl twenty-five years ago.

Her voice was bright when she recognized my voice. "Su-san! How *are* you?"

I felt something crumple inside me. The words came out brokenly. "Not so good."

I could hear her breath catch over the phone. She inhaled, then let it out. "What is it? What's the matter?"

"I'm pregnant."

"Oh." The vowel sound she made was filled with empathy, pain, and recognition. It was exactly the sound I needed to hear. *Thank you*, I said silently.

"What will you do?" Her voice was solemn and soft.

"I've got an appointment. On Monday." I didn't say the word out loud.

"Ah. Well, I think that's probably the best, isn't it?" She knew that my relationship hadn't turned out to be The One, that I wasn't anticipating a long future together. I'd confided in her just as thoroughly as I had with my best girlfriends.

I sighed. "I'm sure it is. But it's still…hard."

"Of course it is. It must be very hard." I could feel the tenderness coming through the receiver and I closed my eyes. It was as if her palm was on my forehead, stroking it.

"You're lucky that you have this option."

"Yes."

"It's what I would have done, if it had been available to me…" And then she stopped short, realizing what she had just said.

I blinked. I tried to keep my voice steady. "Of course. I know." I was balancing on a tightrope. I wanted this support, this ability to confide in her. I needed her to be my understanding, forgiving mother. And yet she had just told me that she would have killed me if she had had the chance. The rigid voice of the woman in the church basement came back to me. I saw the deadly vacuum cleaner. I thought of coat hangers and bottles of X-labeled poisons. I blinked through tears, harder, and pushed it all away.

She tried to smooth over her own words. "Susan, is there anything you need? Can I do anything for you?"

Come to me, I wanted to say. *Come be with me and hold my hand.* But I couldn't choke the words out. To hear her say no would have been unbearable.

"No," I said. "I'm sure it will all be fine."

Maybe she was just echoing my words four years later, telling me what she thought I wanted to hear.

———

I have two other children now, daughters. After losing Samuel, I was frightened and alarmed at my body's betrayal. My husband and I began pursuing adoption instead; it seemed safer than running the gauntlet of another pregnancy. But our two daughters insisted on showing up in our family, despite our feeble efforts at contraception; I am infinitely grateful that they did.

And yet I do not forget that son, small cowboy, the way he galloped through me. Nor do I forget the microscopic, unnamed seahorse of a child who came before that. There is still a part of me that believes that I failed the test of motherhood, the law that says your child comes before you, even if it means death. I put myself first when it came to Samuel, just as she had with me. And sometimes I cannot bear what that feels like. I look at my girls, the life that fills this family, and I think, none of this would be here if I had chosen differently.

If I had stayed with that old boyfriend and never had that first abortion. If I had refused to give up on Samuel's chances. Maybe I wouldn't be here today. Maybe I would have a severely disabled son. If my birth mother had taken a coat hanger to me instead of hiding me under a girdle and then delivering me in a far-away state. If she had stolen away with me and pretended to be a widow in a new town. If that married man, my birth father, had left his wife and children. If, if, if.

There are lifetimes of ifs to consider. But in the end, my birth mother and I made the choices we did. One time I chose one way, and another time it felt less like a choice than a gun at my head.

I am inching toward fifty now. I no longer condemn her or myself for what we decided for ourselves, years ago. Did we choose wrongly? Were we selfish? There is no way to truly answer those questions. My life has been steeped in the tea of reproductive choice since the moment of my own conception. I wish us peace for all that we have chosen.

Susan Ito is the author of *The Mouse Room*, a SheBooks minimemoir. She coedited the literary anthology *A Ghost at Heart's Edge: Stories & Poems of Adoption* (North Atlantic Books). She is a creative nonfiction editor at the online literary journal *Literary Mama*, and her work has appeared in *Growing Up Asian American, Choice, Hip Mama, The Bellevue Literary Review, Making More Waves,* and elsewhere. She has performed her solo show, *The Ice Cream Gene*, around the United States. She writes and teaches at the San Francisco Writers' Grotto, at UC Berkeley Extension, and the MFA program at Bay Path College. Her website is http://susanito.com.

Story Reflection Questions

1. What is one moment in the story that stayed with you?

     _____

     _____

     _____

2. What questions did you find yourself asking as you read the story?

     _____

     _____

     _____

3. What challenged you about the story?

     _____

     _____

     _____

4. What surprised you about the story?

     _____

     _____

     _____

5. How does this story relate to your own life experience?

     _____

     _____

     _____

Childless by Choice

Monica McLemore

"My fullest concentration of energy is available to me only when I integrate all the parts of who I am, openly, allowing power from particular sources of my living to flow back and forth freely through all my different selves, without the restrictions of externally imposed definition. Only then can I bring myself and my energies as a whole to the service of those struggles which I embrace as part of my living."
—Audre Lorde

I never wanted children, and I knew this at a very young age. I have also never been pregnant. There is irony in this statement because for the last twenty-three years as a nurse I have helped other women start their families or helped them end their unintended pregnancies. My perspective on parenthood and children was and continues to be framed by the simple principle that people who know they are not going to be good parents shouldn't parent. I have always appreciated that I came to this perspective early on in life. As I've aged and gained a greater understanding of myself and how I want to exist in the world, I've found it is the most simple and parsimonious way to explain my childless state to those who feel entitled to question it.

I am a black woman who knew at age eight that I wanted to be a nurse. I love nursing and I love being in service to others; I am grateful that I get to do so in such vulnerable moments as when people interact with the health-care system. Outside of a stint working at the mall during high school, I have only worked in health care, and so my early views of being an adult and a woman in the world have been carefully examined through the lens of the experiences of others. Three women (all deceased) have played and continue to play a large role in how I construct my life. These women all contribute to the complexity of who I am, who I strive to be, and represent for me foundational role models as activist and dancer (Josephine Baker), feminist (Simone de Beauvoir), and nurse (Florence Nightingale). None of these women ever gave birth to a child.

Josephine Baker had an emergency hysterectomy after suffering several miscarriages and developing severe pelvic infections that caused scarring of her uterus (peritonitis/septicemia) and went on to adopt and raise twelve children, known as her "rainbow" tribe. Known for her scandalous banana dance in 1925, she stunned the world with her erotic dance shows and her love for pets and eccentric wild animals. To this day, she remains the only black woman and person born in the United States to ever have a full military funeral in France. At one point in her life, Josephine was the richest and most famous black woman on earth, but her accomplishment that inspires me most was her joining the resistance during World War II and filtering secrets to the French Army to help defeat Hitler and the scourge of fear, hate, and xenophobia spreading across most of Europe. I still think it was brilliant of her to fearlessly use her privilege and influence to help stop evil while continuing to be extravagant and glamorous and never apologizing for why the arts, dance, and music matter. Like Josephine, my wish is to take my last breath dancing to music that moves me.

Simone de Beauvoir, the French existentialist who provided the world with *The Second Sex*, ended up adopting a daughter who became her literary heir. Her writings have greatly influenced my thinking about being a woman in the world and the impact of parenthood on one's existence. I have marveled at her ability to fully document her life, including her thoughts, her experiences, and her interactions with others. I always found it particularly striking that as an intellectual woman surrounded by contemporary male intellectuals, she always seemed to be having more fun than most. I have enjoyed both her fiction (*The Mandarins* and *Memoires of a Dutiful Daughter* are particular favorites) and philosophical works that provide for me the example of the kind of scholarly life I aspire to have: great adventures, great loves, and great work.

Finally, Florence Nightingale, "The Lady with the Lamp," came from a wealthy family. She bucked the traditional life that was established for her and headed to the Crimean War. Her epidemiologic study of the environment of care necessary for healing and rehabilitation is still in use today. At the age of thirty-six, she "retired" to her bedroom and prolifically wrote until her death at age ninety. She never married and never had children. *Notes on Nursing*, her seminal text, changed my entire view of how I would relate to people throughout my life and how I conceptualize how to be most effective as a nurse and continues to direct my choices about projects I work on. *Notes on Nursing* taught me one of the most pivotal lessons that guide my work today: It's not about you; it's always about the patients. One of the reasons that my work in abortion, contraception, and family planning care is guided by the concept that "women know best" is because I truly believe this without hesitation. My philosophical orientation to care provision that is grounded in the idea that "it's never about me; it's always about the patients" allows me to accept disparate views that women express within the reproductive rights/justice community without judgment or blame. My job when women need abortions is to provide them excellent care, and this perspective allows me to care for any woman needing one, irrespective of why she needs it.

Pregnancy is an experience that has a lifelong impact on women, and the decision to become a parent or not is one of the most important choices women can make; for me, this was a serious consideration that required careful examination and deliberate decision-making. I knew as a child of the '80s, coming of age at a time when MTV was launched, when the so-called "Mommy Wars" were raging, and when federal and state policies were less than welcoming to working moms and other women in the workplace, I would have to develop a firm resolve and a thick skin around my lack of desire to be a parent. None of these things specifically impacted my decision to remain childless, but collectively, they contributed to an environment that I found to be hostile to women who wanted to parent, while touting multiple opportunities and choices, contributing to a perfection and "having it all" assimilation narrative that I believe is dangerous and unfair.

As a middle child who has two older sisters, I had the opportunity to observe how people responded to my siblings' decisions about parenthood. I have a sister who is ten years older than I am, and also childless, who has a PhD in pharmaceutical chemistry. My other sister, who is five years older than I am, is a successful nonprofit fundraising executive with two children. My brother, who is two years younger than I am, has two children. I enjoy being an aunt and feel that my life is richer because I do have the opportunity to be around the children of my siblings. I can also say with unwavering certainty that I could not and would not have the patience, fortitude, or desire to live with children, and the world is better that I know this fact. I mention my siblings not because their choices to parent or not had any real impact on my choice to remain childless, but because of my parents' reactions to their decisions and my decision to construct my life without children.

From a very young age, I heard the narrative of my parents' experiences with their own parents and families, and two things were very clear to me: first, as a woman, I would have a long, hard path because of my desire not to parent (or that eventually I'd change my mind), and second, that "someone" was responsible for giving my parents grandchildren. I never internalized these messages as being directly applicable to me and am very grateful for that. One of the luxuries of being a middle child is that someone always goes before you. Additionally, my brother, the only person thought capable of continuing the family surname, was mandated to reproduce as the only male. Adding to this middle-child experience was the fact that I knew my grandparents, who lived and died while I was a young adolescent/woman, and had enough extended family that reinforced the idea that the life I imagined for myself was very different than the one that everyone else attempted to foist onto me. I knew when family members asked me about my future that it was best to be as vague as possible and to change the conversation as soon as I could. To this day, I still get extremely frustrated when extended family members who do not have the authority or credibility to comment on my life or choices nevertheless feel very comfortable doing so. I have also learned that much of this concern stems from the fact that they don't want to see me unhappy or tormented by my lack of the visible spoils of socially acceptable lives for women, namely a husband and children.

My father and his two siblings were left in the care of his mother when his father left when he was a very young boy. Being from a "broken home" had a huge impact on my father, and he felt very comfortable retelling his story about how he decided to parent. He was very fond of saying that he always wanted to have a son that he would never abandon and that he would be the kind of father he wished he'd had.

For a black man in the late 1970s and early 1980s, the context of this statement cannot and should not be minimized. While the media began to print stories about the "crack epidemic," HIV infections killed many black men, and the mass incarceration of black men grew exponentially, this trifecta created and reinforced a perception that there was a dearth of marriageable black men and a flight of black men from their families. However, this idea is exclusionary and perpetuates many myths and stereotypes about the preferences that men have for male children. Given that my father already had a daughter from his first marriage and two from his second, it always left me wondering how he conceptualized our existence. It would be another twenty years before I could ask him this question and get a reasonable answer. I had my first taste of sexism, patriarchy, and disparate treatment in my own home; it was helpful that I did because I quickly saw through my family dynamic and spent time listening and observing to hone my emotional and verbal responses to this type of immature and shallow treatment.

Juxtapose this dynamic with my mother, a woman who worked her way up the corporate ladder to retire as vice president of a large regional financial institution while raising three children and always telling me I could do whatever I wanted and be whatever I dreamed of being. I spent a lot of time in my adolescence angry at my parents because this obvious dichotomy of treatment seemed dated. What I later realized after interviewing them for my bachelor's thesis is that they decided a distribution of work needed to occur in their approach to child-rearing given that they both worked. It seems like they made the right choice—they've been married for fifty years.

My relationship with my parents throughout my twenties, after finishing college, was horrible, and I accept some of the blame for this fact. I moved to

California shortly after college for many reasons, but primarily I didn't want to continue to live in the shadow of my parents. My parents were well known in the small city where I grew up. I chose a college down the road from where my parents still live and my first job as a nurse was in the hospital I was born in, right after college. I needed my world to be bigger. Similar to Josephine Baker, I packed my bags and went to a place that welcomed me with open arms: for her, France—for me, San Francisco.

I would return to the east coast three or four times per year to see my siblings and my parents, and after each visit I felt like I was being judged for wasting my "good" years. Throughout my twenties, family members felt OK questioning me about my life, my partners, and my plans, and it never dawned on me not to answer! I am offended at how many times during my twenties I was asked when I would settle down, find a nice man, and have some children. I argued with anyone and everyone about this, working through my thoughts in conversation as I still do. "I have a legitimate life" or "It won't be the worst thing if I never get married," I would bark.

I even judged my mom for her relationship with my dad and on several occasions called him a misogynist bigot in her presence. The last time this happened was when my father called me joyously when my nephew (now ten years old) was born, screaming, "He's here, he's here," and I kept thinking to myself, *I have never seen him that animated about anything I've ever done, misogynist bigot.* And I hung up the phone.

Matters weren't helped much by my complete abandonment of the evangelical upbringing that my parents exposed me to. I became an atheist. I immersed myself in the writings of de Beauvoir, Sartre, and Camus and decided that an existential approach to life would best suit me.

My twenties were a tumultuous time, and I spent a lot of time and money in therapy, mostly as an exercise in self-exploration, doing deep work to understand how and why I as a nurse could be such an angry person; I was attempting to reconcile my ability to care for absolute strangers while at the same time never wanting to speak to my blood relatives.

I decided in my late twenties and thirties that I needed to focus and return to school if I wanted to do the kind of work I dreamed of doing. My birthday falls on New Year's Eve, and Y2K happened when I was turning thirty. I spent most of 1999 in reflection, considering choices I had made much earlier in my life. Florence Nightingale's use of epidemiology intrigued me, and her ability to comprehend the environment of care and translate that to nursing practice motivated me to pursue my master's in public health as opposed to a master's in nursing. During my MPH studies, I quickly realized I'd need to advance my education, so I applied to PhD programs.

Throughout my life, I've always had an active social and dating life. And during graduate school this was especially true. Not having or wanting children opens a wide range of possibilities when seeking sexual pleasure or love, and I think uncoupling those things from childbearing afforded me experiences I probably would not otherwise have had. I am fortunate to have experienced many types of love from people with different gender identities and racial backgrounds. I had great loves during the decade I was in graduate school and, not known to many, I was briefly married and divorced. Graduate school changed me in ways I never anticipated, but I never changed my mind about children. It was during my PhD program that my relationship with my parents deteriorated, and I believe part of that was attributable to my declining fertility and their need to accept that perhaps me "changing my mind about parenting" wasn't going to happen. It was also during this time that my siblings had their children and my parents were otherwise preoccupied with being grandparents.

It was not until my forties, when I was preparing to defend my dissertation, that my relationship with my parents improved. It felt like finishing my degree finally provided them with something I had done that they could be proud of that was tangible to other people. I have never asked them if that is true, but I will. They have been married for fifty years, and in all of my conversations with them and reflecting on how my relationship with them has changed over time, I do admire their ability to accept each other as they are, and now I finally feel like they accept me the way I am, childless by choice.

———

Dr. Monica McLemore is an assistant professor in the Family Health Care Nursing Department at the University of California, San Francisco, and a clinician-scientist at Advancing New Standards in Reproductive Health, a program of the Bixby Center for Global Reproductive Health. Her research interests include unintended pregnancy prevention, the efficacy and safety of nurse-administered procedural sedation, tumor markers of ovarian cancer and their behavior across the menstrual cycle, the nursing role in abortion care provision, and pilot testing of a doula training program as a job vocational program for previously incarcerated women. Dr. McLemore has a BS in nursing from the College of New Jersey, an MPH from San Francisco State University, and a PhD from the University of California, San Francisco School of Nursing.

Story Reflection Questions

1. What is one moment in the story that stayed with you?

   _____

   _____

   _____

2. What questions did you find yourself asking as you read the story?

   _____

   _____

   _____

3. What challenged you about the story?

   _____

   _____

   _____

4. What surprised you about the story?

   _____

   _____

   _____

5. How does this story relate to your own life experience?

   _____

   _____

   _____

Donation

Ashley Talley

My mother and I have been speaking in numbers.

We know that HCG levels determine pregnancy. In the beginning, fifty is good. A reading above twenty-five makes you a mother, but below five, you are not. After three weeks, you should reach one thousand. When your HCG level is one thousand early on, you can picture your wide, white-mooned stomach. You can buy pants with elastic ovals in front from the maternity store at the mall and maybe stick a few paint swatches with names like cherub pink and mountain bluebell in your purse. When you have a thousand, you are winning.

We have become mathematicians, scientists, and experts on the percentages of possibility: fertility rates, hormonal drugs, eggs, sperm, cycles. Before, we knew that the first baby created through in vitro fertilization was born in 1978 only because we remembered it from *Jeopardy*. But now we spit out facts: 1984—birth year of the first baby resulting from egg transfer; 40,000—the estimated number of children born through assisted reproductive therapy last year; and 15,000—the dollars my mother and her husband spend on each round of fertility treatment.

My mother is forty-seven. She has been pregnant five times in her life, but I am an only child and, ironically, a result of the only pregnancy she didn't plan. After finding out she was going to have a baby as a twenty-year-old junior in college, she chose to postpone graduation and marry my father, a fun-loving, football-playing frat boy. Three years, one child, and one miscarriage later, they went through a mostly amicable divorce, and Mama devoted the next fifteen years of her life to me. Our world never seemed small nor our lives unfulfilled, and I understood the word *family* to mean a planet of two people, a woman and a girl, who didn't need the orbits of second husbands or distant relatives, and certainly not of other children, to make it spin happily through the universe. Though she dated very little throughout my childhood, I never heard Mama mention being lonely.

When I left for college, she began a tumultuous relationship with Forrest, a man I met before she did through the martial arts classes we both took at our small town's karate studio. He was an artist twelve years younger than her, blond and sweet-faced and closer to my age than my mother's. A mutual friend, also in that karate class, introduced them at the gym, and they fell in love slowly, over old movies and gourmet meals. From the beginning, I knew he was a complicated person, introverted yet friendly, passionate yet occasionally passive. Though I didn't really come to know him then, and perhaps don't even now, I could tell that he was good and kind. Though the next few years of the relationship's turmoil often challenged that estimation of his character, I trusted and believed in those two qualities completely.

When my mother loves, she loves hard, and the first time that Forrest broke up with her, she became a depressed and despondent woman I didn't recognize. During the subsequent breakups, I helped her sweep the shattered pieces of herself into piles she could reconstruct later, but every time she seemed mended or nearly happy, Forrest came back into her life and the cycle began again. Finally, after five years and a thousand ups and downs, he said the words she had wanted to hear all her life: "I love you. I want you to be my wife and the mother of my children." And with this definitive declaration, that on-and-off relationship turned into the most stable and happy of marriages, missing only one aspect to make it complete for my mother: a child.

Mama is one for five in her attempts to have a baby. That's a 20 percent success rate—only marginally lower than the 26 percent of couples who have a child through in vitro fertilization, which was the first infertility treatment she and my stepfather tried. Since that initial attempt, they have moved on to assisted reproductive technology and egg donation, which have significantly higher success rates. In what now seems a strange and complicated twist of events, my eggs were the first my mother used to chemically conceive.

My mother is the person I'm closest to in the world, but our lives have often moved in opposition to one another. The more she trusts her choices, the less I seem able to believe in my own. Just as her life was falling into place—an engagement, a beautiful new Victorian home, an unexpected but hoped-for pregnancy—mine seemed to be falling apart. I realize now I resented her and Forrest for the hands they held in public and the private way she whispered to him during a play or church service. Love notes meant for his lunch bag ended up on the kitchen table, and the boxer shorts and lacy bras that appeared in our shared laundry annoyed and embarrassed me.

Mama got pregnant naturally at the age of forty-three, a few months before the huge June wedding she and Forrest had planned for three hundred guests. Still bearing a certain amount of Southern Baptist guilt and fearing the months counted backward by their friends and very traditional family, they were married secretly and quietly by Mama's best friend's father, a judge who was the first person outside of my family to hold me after my birth.

A few months after that quiet March ceremony, Mama had a miscarriage, and she walked down the center aisle of the church on the arm of her father—beautiful, happy, and a little desperate for what she's told me. "You'll understand when you meet someone you really love. You'll want to create life with them."

At that point, my life seemed far from any understanding of love and miles from the idea of procreation. After my college graduation and a stint as an editorial intern with a travel magazine, I moved back to our small town, ostensibly to teach ninth-grade English at the high school I'd attended and where my mother still taught, but mostly to move in with my boyfriend, a beautiful anomaly of a man whom I never really understood. Forrest and Sean could not have been more different. Where my boyfriend was strong in will, my stepfather was strong in heart, and each had faults the other one lacked. My mother was always wary of Sean's charm.

He was a college dropout who regularly beat me at Trivial Pursuit, a former model who then became a roofer. He read philosophy books for hours before meeting me at a bar for tequila shots and dancing, where he bought beers and told jokes to men whose faces he would later shatter in the parking lot over imagined or exaggerated insults. Though he lacked softness, I appreciated his intensity, intelligence, and passion. But after we moved in together, a step my mother warned me against, those tequila shots turned into Budweisers before noon, and the Nietzsche tomes became heavy objects thrown angrily against a wall. By the time I acknowledged the alcoholism, drug use, unfaithfulness, and emotional abuse, things were broken that could not be fixed, and I realized he was not someone, in my mother's measure of real love, with whom I could ever create a life.

When the world came crashing down on me one late night in early July, my mother was on a belated honeymoon, and it was my father, in town for Independence Day, who saw the bruises at my throat and wrist and went with me to gather my belongings from the house I shared with Sean. I went to Mama's house that morning to be alone, and the rooms were quiet and empty with the gray light of dawn filtering through her curtains. I called the house where she and Forrest were vacationing, but when she answered, I hung up quickly and hiccupped short breaths between sobs. When I called back hours later, I was calmer, and I explained what had happened.

"Well, we'll come home," she said, and even in her thick, sleep-filled voice, I noticed her "I" was already firmly a "we."

"No," I said. "It's fine. I'm OK." My voice maintained a calm I didn't feel.

"We can pack up right now and be there in five hours," she offered repeatedly.

But I found myself unwilling to express to her the terror of the situation I'd just experienced or to even show her the desperation and loneliness I was feeling in those moments. "No, I'm fine. Enjoy the rest of your honeymoon," I told her, getting off the phone quickly. I was angry at my mother for not being there exactly when I needed her most, and I wouldn't share this grief with her. I wouldn't even show her the injuries.

Like the long sleeves I wore for weeks, the faces I put on that summer were meant to hide or distract from the reality of my life. If my mother laughed at a family dinner, I turned away and gazed to the floor stonily, and if she tried to have a serious conversation with me, I smiled at her gravity and walked away. "Whatever, Mom," I said, rolling my eyes like a thirteen-year-old brat. "Just chill out." I kept the emotions I was feeling as carefully hidden as the rough scabs and fading bruises on my skin.

I turned away from Mama as I never had before or have since. I felt she had taken away my family, that small orbit that before meant mother and daughter, and I accused her of callousness, selfishness, and inconsideration of my feelings. I would not accept or even try to understand the shifting groundwork in this woman who had always been my stability and my home. I was floating through my own world, untethered and scared, and though she had supported me through four years at Brown, six months in Europe, and another five in Alabama, she seemed to have let go. She could not hold me, or would not. The strength of connection that had always bound us, perhaps since it was a physical cord umbilically attached from her body to mine, seemed to have disappeared, and I felt its absence as absolutely as an amputation.

I moved to Philadelphia with my best friend and stayed at another girlfriend's house when I visited home. We still talked nearly every day, though I kept my half of the conversation mostly on the surface. "Work's fine. Yeah, we saw a movie tonight. I don't know when I'm off for Christmas. How is everybody? Great." But after long, strained months when she tried to reconnect with me, my iciness slowly melted, and I went to her, as I always have, with my questions and fears. Things returned to normal between Mama, Forrest, and me, or perhaps life just settled into what it would become. I knew that, above all else, my mother still wanted to conceive a child with her husband, and they were already in touch with Duke Fertility Center by the end of that year, 2003.

Oddly, neither my mother nor I can quite remember when I became involved in her quest for a baby. Mama locates the conversation during the brief time I lived in Philadelphia, perhaps over the weekend that she, Forrest, and some other family members came up to see me in a production of *Steel Magnolias*, where I played Annelle, the devout Christian hairdresser portrayed by Darryl Hannah in the movie. In the final act, after a quick change when the stagehands stuffed a large pillow under my dress, I walked on stage nine months pregnant, pushing at my lower back and softly rubbing my stomach, the way every movie-mother-to-be does. My family laughed and clapped at my performance, but I recognized the falseness and absurdity of the situation. My mother desperately wanted that swollen thrill of pregnancy I was portraying on stage, but my own life, so unsettled and nomadic, was far from its actuality. I felt like a girl playing a woman, a daughter pretending to be a mother.

Mama says my role in her attempt at pregnancy arose not long after that performance, but my most vivid memory of it is a few months later over scratchy phone lines between Southeast Asia and her house in southern Virginia. After saving up money from my office job in Philadelphia, I moved to Kuala Lumpur, Malaysia, in January of 2004 to live with my aunt and uncle. I spent the next months exploring the region and managed calls home every week or two. But still, neither Mama nor I are certain who first brought up the idea. Neither of us seems willing now to claim its instigation, and this ambiguity lends a sense of inevitability to the situation.

Her older sister wasn't able to have children, and Mama always said she'd be willing to be a surrogate if Gwen wanted her to. Perhaps it was during one of these discussions that the topic of donation was first broached. "Well, could Gwen donate eggs to you guys, or is that not how it works?" I asked uncertainly.

"No. Women over forty have something like twenty-five percent the chance of having healthy, viable eggs as women in their thirties, and I think it goes down about the same into the twenties. Most egg donors are in college, I think."

"Yeah, I remember those weird ads in the college newspaper offering thousands of dollars for eggs. It's so strange." The phone line, so many thousands of miles long, was silent, and it seemed wrong to attach monetary value to this life my mother wanted so badly to create. "Well, Mom," I said, using a nomenclature I know she doesn't like, "I'm only twenty-four. I mean, I could do it if you guys needed someone."

There must have been a pause there, long, breathy seconds when we both adjusted to the idea and the choices it would involve. I pictured Mama's face, and Forrest's, and my own. I thought of a puzzle with pieces that necessarily overlapped to form the right picture. Ideas of heroism or altruism or redemption passed through me but never became reasons or motivation I could clearly state. But during those long moments, everything seemed to settle in, rightly, between us, and the strange construction of this new idea came to feel something like another type of cord—a link not just between me, my mother, and this unformed child, but also between the person I had been and the person I could be. The baby, the girl, the daughter, the sister, and the mother. I can't say exactly what Mama thought of the plan, though we agree neither of us questioned its plausibility.

For the next weeks after that, as Mama and Forrest continued to make plans with Duke's fertility specialists, there was a repetition of variants on the same conversation. "Are you sure, Ashley?" she would ask over and over. "Because you don't have to. I don't want to put any pressure on you." I remember short, weighty pauses as I ran my fingernails along the creases in the dark wooden floors of my aunt's house. It was still so outrageous an idea, particularly from our distance almost directly across the world from one another, that I didn't really know what to say.

Because then, and even now sometimes, the whole thing seemed like science fiction, or a strange, futuristic plot twist dreamed up by Rod Serling. I was offering to donate eggs to my mother, which would be added to her husband's sperm, and then implanted in my mother. She would carry and deliver the child, and they would have a baby with the closest possible match to her own DNA. She would have her dream then, and her family, and perhaps then one of us would be tethered to something strong and rooted.

"No, Mom, I'm sure," I told her in different ways, again and again. "I wouldn't have offered if I didn't mean it. I don't have to do much, right? It's just…I mean, it's just like some shots and a short…procedure, right?" My vocabulary didn't include a lexicon with which to talk about these events and neither did my emotions. I could only express things in the negative: "No, I'm not scared. I'm not unsure. I'm not nervous. I don't think I'll feel weird or care later or have issues. No, I don't want you to use someone you don't know." I found it difficult to define the reasons behind my choice, and it was hard to reassure Mama of my certainty without this vocabulary.

I didn't know how to say it, but some small, locked part of myself was sure the decision was right. I wanted to offer this gift to my mother and her husband, this tangible chance at life was certainly the ultimate present. I like to give thoughtful gifts—knitted scarves, arranged weekend get-aways, or hand-painted wineglasses for Christmas presents—but I sometimes wonder if my offerings are more selfish than altruistic. I wonder if it's gratitude I confuse with love or the recognition and affirmation of my goodness I desire over real esteem. I continually seek approval, and in some way, perhaps this procedure was to ensure that my mother, whose opinion has always mattered most, never doubted me and was always a little indebted to me.

Looking back now, I also wonder if my choice to donate eggs to my mother and stepfather had little to do with the conception of a child or the creation of a new family. That spring of 2004, I was living a life of flux. I seemed to be between so many things—jobs, relationships, homes—and I was looking for some footing or grounding in my life. I needed something to hold me somewhere, and this process provided a connection not only to people, but to a place. To complete the donation project, I had to be within a few hours of Duke for the regular exams and procedures, and by living in my mother's house, I didn't have to pay rent or explain to a roommate what the vials in the refrigerator were for or why I stuck a needle into my stomach daily. For all my gypsy ambition, I realized I wanted to be needed, and moving back home and helping my mother have a baby offered me a temporary purpose as I struggled to find my own.

One aspect of the project that preoccupied me from the beginning was the math and chemistry of the whole thing: if I'm half my mother and half my father, and if the baby is half my DNA and half Forrest's, then one fourth of the new life we're creating is chemically my father. I pictured my dad's loud, stubborn strength, his rollicking energy and raucous stories, and then I thought of my stepfather's deliberate way of going about the world, of his soft, cheerful voice and artist's hands. What sort of person, what face, would emerge from such strange roots? The branches of this family tree were tangled and complicated, and I've learned since then that many health systems don't allow daughter-to-mother donation because of such complexities. But as we navigated the twisted corridors of Duke Hospital on my first visit there, the situation didn't feel outlandish or wrong.

Mama and Forrest led me into the narrow, dim waiting room of the fertility center, and they greeted Teresa, one of the head nurses, by name. I filled out long forms about my health and family history, and we were taken back into a small room. Dr. Price, an awkward but polite young physician, went over the basics of the process with us, and I felt my mother glancing at me from time to time, trying to gauge my reaction to the information.

Donation

In his nasal Southern accent, he explained the drugs we would be taking and their various effects of readying my mother's body for pregnancy, temporarily suppressing the functions of both our ovaries, and eventually hyperstimulating the egg production in mine. He mentioned the single shot of HCG I would be given when an ultrasound showed I was ready, and he emphasized the importance of a strict schedule and timetable for administering the drugs. The normalcy with which he and his assistants treated and talked about these procedures reinforced my decision, and when Molly, a pretty young nurse whom we all liked, took us to another room to show us how to give ourselves the shots, we might have been in a cooking or yoga class for all the ease and humor involved in our lesson. As we stuck saline-filled syringes first in oranges and then in the pinched-up skin of our stomachs, Mama said, "Maybe this is something you'd like to do. Something like Molly?" I had recently mentioned perhaps going back to school for medicine, and at that moment, with a future we thought would be filled by the miracles of science, working with infertile couples seemed a natural, suitable option.

"Yeah, maybe so," I answered, feeling the harmless liquid spread beneath my skin as I pressed the end of the syringe toward my body.

Over the next months, Mama and I made the hour-long trip to Durham several times a week, undergoing numerous physicals, blood tests, and ultrasounds. Egg donors normally go through a psychiatric evaluation with the hospital's clinical psychologist, but because I was not an anonymous donor and had discussed everything with my mother and stepfather, Dr. Price said we could forego that technicality.

One of the major decisions we were asked to make over the extended consultations with various experts was whether or not we would tell the child about its origin. After a lot of discussion when we all tried to silently gauge what the other two were thinking, we decided that we wouldn't tell the child unless it—he, she, possibly they—found out on its own. In fact, we decided to tell no one about the procedure, which made for some interesting explanations to friends about the syringes in the backseat of my car. That choice felt right to me though, because I did consider what we were producing as Mama and Forrest's child. "I'm not having the baby," I said on multiple occasions. "I'm just helping out with the biology."

The biology and chemistry turned out to be fairly complicated in itself, however. My mother and I became smart in ways never required by our literary occupations. We learned to say "sub-q" for shots given just under the skin and "IM" for the intramuscular ones that had to be injected by another person. We knew the value—monetary and emotional—of estrogen patches and alcohol swabs and needles and birth control pills and regulated cycles. We would have been brilliant addicts, had we been another type of woman, knowing as we did the exact angle at which to inject ourselves and the softest part of the lower back to inject each other.

But, as with anything one does over and over, these once-foreign practices became part of our household routine. It was not unusual to walk in the kitchen and see my mother's pajama top pulled up and Forrest behind her, wincing more than she was, as he tried to give the IM shot where it would cause the least pain. In front of the refrigerator, I would quickly and painlessly jab in the syringe of hormones, just above the waistband of the black pants I wore to my waitressing job. It was nearly summer by then, and I was determined not to let what was happening at home affect the rhythm of my life. I still went out drinking with my friends after work and lay by the pool, slightly swollen in my bikini from the daily injections of Follistim. Though I wasn't seriously dating anyone, I knew that I couldn't have sex until after the retrieval since I was off birth control and extremely fertile—we hoped.

When an ultrasound showed that my eggs were numerous and ready, they set a morning in late May for the "retrieval," a procedure during which the eggs are extracted through a long needle that is inserted into the follicles of the ovaries. I don't remember much of the experience, especially after the IV was in my arm and anesthesia fogged my consciousness. I know I was ready for it though, after feeling discombobulated, swollen, and slightly crazy for the past few months. I was ready to regain my own balance. Since beginning the donation process, my moods had been erratic, and I was easily irritated. I had also stopped taking the antidepressants that had helped me through the previous months, and the more time went by, stirrings of that old resentment toward my mother and her new life began to reappear. Again, I felt myself untethered, without a real home, and now with a body and temperament I couldn't predict. By the day of the retrieval, I was ready to be done.

I remember nothing of the procedure itself, though it is supposedly very painful if the anesthesia wears off. The nurses gave me pills for any residual pain, and I slept in the backseat on the way home. I had arranged to meet an old friend from college in Baltimore for a baseball game the same afternoon, and I wouldn't let the idea go, even after my mother's worried cautions. The retrieval had been successful, yielding twelve or fifteen eggs, and Mama and Forrest, tentative and thankful, gave me their car and gas money for the six-hour drive.

"You know how much this means to me, don't you?" she asked me, tightly holding my body against hers before I left. "You know how much we appreciate all you've done for us." There were tears in her voice, but all I did was nod, get in the car, and drive away.

After hours of Darvosets and driving, I nearly got sick that night on the way to Georgetown, but something drove me to continue the weekend trip we had planned. I needed to assert my independence from the situation my mother, her husband, and I had just gone through; I needed to step away and let the rest happen to them and not to me. I was happy about what I had offered Mama and Forrest, proud that I could help them gain something so monumental, but now I needed the story to be their own. I wanted my involvement to be over and my life to go back to normal. I was ready to take on the role of daughter wholeheartedly, and leave that strange, murky question of "mother" far behind.

I was traveling again a few weeks after the successful fertilization and implanting of several eggs. I was heading south this time when Mama called me crying. She tried to talk but quickly handed the phone to Forrest.

"Hey, Ashley," he said in a voice I've never heard rise above calm. "Teresa just called, and the pregnancy test came back."

He was quiet for a second, but with Mama's reaction, I felt like I didn't even need to ask the question. "And, well, it's complicated you know, like all this stuff is. She's technically pregnant, but the HCG numbers are really low, and they think it's just a chemical pregnancy."

I sighed slowly and said, "Well, there are still some frozen eggs, right? So they can use those, right, and try again?"

"Yeah, yeah. I'm not sure when that will be, but we're not giving up!" His optimism tried desperately to crawl over my mother's tears, and I guess he mostly succeeded because when she called me back a few hours later, her voice was clear and stable.

"I guess it's not true what they say, is it? 'You're either pregnant or you're not.'" She laughed and I tried to join her. "There is an in between!"

That fall, I moved to coastal North Carolina and began graduate school. In September, Mama and Forrest used the final three fertilized eggs that had been frozen earlier in the spring. They waited tentatively for the numbers again and were finally sure enough to call and tell me they were pregnant. A few months went by, hopeful and thankfully uneventful, until I was eventually ready to believe it myself. We were all so happy through Thanksgiving and early December, and they planned a special Christmas Eve dinner to tell their parents. Envelopes addressed to "Grandma and Grandpa" waited on their fine china with tiny ultrasound pictures inside. While Mama and Forrest clutched each other's hands and I stood in the doorway with my best friend, our family opened their cards and various shrieks erupted after a few moments of confused silence.

"Look at that!" Forrest's mother shouted to his father. "That's my grandchild! My first grandchild. Look at that!"

As they moved around the table, hugging and congratulating one another, I turned to my friend and asked her which bar she wanted to go to that night. When my grandmother came over and put her arm around me, she asked, "And how do you feel about being a big sister for the first time?"

I shrugged off her embrace, smiled without teeth, and said something noncommittal. "Yeah, that's crazy isn't it?" I grabbed my coat and bag, refusing the bread pudding and coffee Mama was offering, and my friend and I left for Hill's Tavern. No one else knew of my involvement in the pregnancy, and, walking away again, I tried to deny the connection too. A part of me wondered if all the years ahead would be like this. Was my place in this new life and new family that of a bystander? Would I always be on the fringes now, a shadow in the doorway, waiting to leave? How would this child consider me as it grew? Was it simply biology I had helped my mother with, as I assured her? My knowledge of the truth behind this new baby rendered the whole celebration absurd and a little heartbreaking, but I hoped I was the only one who felt that way.

Three days later, Mama had a miscarriage. She cried on the couch for several days, and I sat in the chair beside her, feeling weird, guilty, sad, and, in a small way, relieved. It was not a person I had known or a life I had felt, though technically, perhaps, it should have been. I did not know how to grieve for a death that was not quite death, from a life that was not quite life. I didn't know where to put the child in my own story, and so I stepped away and tried to distance myself from what I could not talk about or understand.

To me, it felt like both a failure and a victory. I felt responsible, in an irrational way, for the failure of the pregnancy, as though my eggs weren't quite good enough to survive. Perhaps it was one too many glasses of wine, I thought, or the cigarettes I still smoked sporadically that killed this thing that would have been a person. In another way, though, a piece of me was glad that we would not have to deal with the questions and complications that would inevitably arise as the child grew up. We would never have to consider what the words *mother, daughter,* and *sister* actually meant in relation to us.

But the feeling that I had let Mama and Forrest down, that I had failed in a very basic way, overrode my relief, and after a few months we agreed to begin the process all over again. During the spring of 2005, I began the drug cycles once more and made the two-hour drive north to Duke several times. On one of those visits, I was asked to sit down and talk with Julia, a vibrant, friendly psychologist employed by the fertility center. She was surprised that I hadn't had to go through the battery of tests on our first go-round, and she insisted that it was necessary this time.

Julia was young and earnest, and after I went through a basic series of psychological and personality tests, we sat in an office and chatted like friends. I was lulled into the conversation, never thinking that it was anything more than a formality. She was particularly interested in my history of depression ("Just situational," I said, waving it away. "I'm fine now.") and in that moment right before the last retrieval when I cried without explanation. I thought I came across calm, informed, and sure of the choice I had made and was making again, so when Julia told Dr. Price that she could not, in good conscience, allow me to donate eggs, I was stunned and irate. I felt that I had been duped and betrayed by this woman, and my anger was so potent I wrote a letter the next day to the head of the center, complaining about her overly easy manner and what I judged to be her gentle manipulation and unwarranted duplicity.

Looking back, I realize that my anger was mostly misguided. I was mad that this choice I had made, willingly and with open eyes, was being taken away from me by a person who had no real relationship to the situation. She removed my role in Mama's quest, effectively severing my connection to the new family my mother was working to create. But really, why should I have had such a direct part in it? I'm sure I knew deep down that Julia was right to stop the donation process, but I resented the confiscation of my choice in the situation. I wanted the right to give this gift to my mother and to be a part of the transformation of my family. But this was a new family, and I did not need to help create it to remain a part of it. I never fully considered the weight my decision might come to bear upon myself, my family, and the new life we were trying so hard to produce, and I understand now it was the choice I didn't make, couldn't make, that was ultimately the right one.

I recently found a journal from the time of the donation process and came across this paragraph: "I find myself unwilling to analyze my situation too much—unwilling to make any sort of actual decision about how I feel, but I guess that's OK—that's how life happens, right? Without our careful orchestration, without even our vaguest say-so." I agree with this past self, I think. Often it's not the choices we make, but the events we cannot control that determine the course of our futures. I like to believe I have power over my life and its paths, but I know that sometimes you need to close your eyes, throw up your hands, and take what comes. And that's a choice too.

Two years after my last visit to the fertility clinic, my involvement in Mama's effort to get pregnant has ended, but she and Forrest are still trying. They have reached their final attempt now, having maxed out credit cards, borrowed from her parents, and taken out a second mortgage on their house. They are using eggs from a donor they will never meet, and they still give shots, take pills, and visit Duke with methodical regularity. Mama is positive when she talks about it even now, sure somehow that if you want something badly enough, if you make choices and sacrifices to get it, then it will become something you can hold.

———

Ashley Talley grew up in southern Virginia and currently lives in eastern North Carolina. She graduated from Brown University with a B.A. in English and honors in creative writing, and received her MFA from UNC Wilmington. After years of writing for magazines and newspapers, Ashley now works in television news. She loves to cook, read, write, travel, play tennis, kayak, hike, play on the beach with her sweet dog Lucy and spend time with her little brother, Joel.

Story Reflection Questions

1. What is one moment in the story that stayed with you?

    _____

    _____

    _____

2. What questions did you find yourself asking as you read the story?

    _____

    _____

    _____

3. What challenged you about the story?

    _____

    _____

    _____

4. What surprised you about the story?

    _____

    _____

    _____

5. How does this story relate to your own life experience?

    _____

    _____

    _____

In an Age of Science

Alisa A. Gaston-Linn

The reaction I received from my family was not what I had expected. My mother told me I should not have a child. "Your life is so good, you have money, a nice home, you take two vacations a year out of the country. Why would you want to do this? You're too old." I questioned myself after this conversation.

I had been single until my late thirties, which I was comfortable with. I wanted to meet a man and have what one thinks a woman would have by her late twenties: a gratifying career, excellent husband, and, of course, children. I had always wanted four kids. As time went on, and I failed to meet the right man, my ideal kid number dropped to two. By the time I met my future husband, I had come to terms with not having children at all and was content with my close relationships with my niece and nephews. But then, one night while lying on the bed talking, my soon-to-be groom asked me if I wanted kids. He said he did, and I thought, the women in my family had no problems getting pregnant. I was healthy, I exercised, I ate nothing but organic. This will happen.

Two weeks after we married I turned forty, and we immediately began trying to get pregnant. My ob-gyn put me on Clomid, a nonsteroidal ovulatory stimulant used to increase the chances of becoming pregnant. I used it for six months. Nothing. Then she told me I needed to see a fertility specialist. I was confused; I thought women went to such doctors only after trying for at least a year. "You're not young. You need help with this."

I spoke to my husband, and we made a list of how far we were willing to go. We had the financial means, so our attitudes were casual. Let's try every option, including adoption, and if it happens, great, if not, we have a good life regardless.

Our fertility doctor and the nurses were amazing: nothing but positive attitudes. They all told us I would be pregnant in no time. My husband's sperm was tested and, according to the experts, he was a "rock star." Of course that was wonderful news, but it was the first unsettling inkling that it was I who could not perform, not him. Not that it mattered, but I felt as though I had failed. I asked myself, what have I done to my body? Is my mother right—am I too old?

During this time, women around me became pregnant. One by one, in the office, I noticed bellies booming, maternity dresses flowing, faces glowing. Some of the women complained. I smiled and supported them, but on the inside I wanted to scream that they should be grateful. At the fertility clinic, we did our first insemination. As I sat in the recovery room, instructed to lie there for twenty minutes, holding my husband's hand, we were excited. And then nothing.

I had dinner with a good friend. She told me she was pregnant. I swelled with genuine happiness for her, but I also felt jealous and envious. She was thirty-eight and she and her husband hadn't wanted children. They changed their minds and it happened right away. We clinked our glasses and celebrated and she told me, "It will happen for you." Feeling her kindness and support relaxed me and flipped the bad feelings I had felt just moments before into hope.

My husband and I did three more inseminations, and with each failure, I began to feel slighter, like a frailty struggling to weather the elements. I remember stopping at a red light in my car one afternoon and looking over to a woman on the curb. She must have been about seventeen or eighteen, she was very pregnant, and she was smoking. I fumed inside. My mother asked me several times why I was doing this to myself. I bucked up, went to my fertility doctor, and asked what was next. He said IVF. I said, "OK, let's do it."

"Great, but we need to use a donor for the eggs."

"Why?"

"Because your eggs are too old."

My stomach dropped and my head ached; it seemed the cruelest of insults. He must have instantly noticed my angst because he responded by saying, "Do you want a fifteen percent chance? Or an eighty-five percent chance?"

I drove home down the long, isolated road with the magnificent Rocky Mountains to the west, and the dry plains to the east, and the memorial sign dedicated to a man who had died on that stretch after a head-on collision with a dump truck. It will not be my baby, I thought to myself. It will not have any part of me. It will be made up of my husband and some stranger. But long roads are magical in the sense that they give more time—more time to weigh options and to morph tumultuous thoughts into regal purity. I realized that if we were to adopt, the child would not be made of me either, and I would love it no matter what. So what was the difference?

My husband agreed. Picking an egg donor was a humbling and bizarre experience. We had a stack of files in front of us, photos of the donors, and sometimes photos of them as babies and of relatives. We read their medical histories. The young woman who admitted to smoking pot on a regular basis was out. The woman who was prone to depression was out. It did not seem fair. I felt judgmental considering that if I were to fill out an application to donate eggs, I would be turned down for having a family history punctured with depression, bipolar disease, addiction, heart attacks, and diabetes. But now we have options.

My husband and I chose a woman we thought might look as though she could fit in with my family. Dark hair, green eyes. She had three children of her own and a beautiful smile. I started the pill so that I would be on the same cycle as her. A few weeks later, our doctor called and told us the donor did not produce enough eggs. Back to the folders. I wanted the woman who was mixed: she had a white mother and black father. She had gorgeous curly hair and looked like my niece. I have naturally curly hair. I thought, if this child doesn't come from my DNA, at least it can have some feature that resembles me. My husband would not do it, and this shocked me. He is a white man from England and is the most open man I've been with as far as accepting all of my friends regardless of their sexual orientation or racial background. He had difficulty articulating why he was so adamant. The way it came out sounded as though he did not want a black baby. I didn't want to believe this, so I pushed for him to explain exactly what he meant, and we argued. "What about when we talked about adopting from China?"

"I didn't want to adopt from China," he said.

Thinking about what he might be holding back horrified me. He struggled to put it into words, but after we quarreled for some time, I finally realized it had nothing to do with race. It had to do with his vision of being a father—his ego. He wanted a baby that looked like him. Anger surged into me. This baby would definitely not look like me, so how dare he be so stubborn and selfish about the baby looking like him?

The conversation further defined my separateness from this possible baby. I became stuck on the fact that I would never look at a small person growing up and into the features of my husband and me. I would be looking at a child that resembled him, or some version of him with another woman. And then I felt mortified, grasping that this was about my ego as well. I lassoed my thoughts again, understanding who I am and knowing for certain that I would love this baby no matter what.

We chose a woman who, amazingly, had the exact heritage as me. German, French, and Native American. She had brown hair and green eyes. Tall, healthy, working on her master's degree. She was single and had had one abortion. We'll take her. When I began the pill again to get into sync with the new donor, I felt some strange sort of connection with her. We are moving into the same space; we are colliding; you are courageous and giving, and I will have a child. I felt pure love for this woman I had never, and would never, meet.

She was able to give us sixteen embryos, eight of which met the criteria to be used. We signed papers. What would we do with the leftover embryos? There were three choices: donation to another couple, donation to science, or embryo cryopreservation for our future use. We were not allowed to donate to another couple because, as our doctor explained, there is now a law that forbids donation by people who are from England or have been to England within a year of creation of the embryos due to mad cow disease. As ridiculous as the law seemed to our doctor and us, we accepted that we could not donate embryos. We knew that it was unlikely we would have another child, so cryo was out. Donation to science. I felt good about the possibility of contributing to the greater good of stem cell research. This could give someone her eyesight back.

A month before the scheduled procedure, we began all the required drugs and hormones to prepare my body—to trick my body into thinking it had released an egg, then accepted it after fertilization, and was now ready to let it embed itself into my womb. I could not bring myself to shove needles into my own skin, so each morning before he left for work, my husband stuck my stomach or thigh with the one-inch needle and released Lupron from the syringe. I also took Estrace orally. Each evening, my husband stuck my hip with the two-inch needle and released the progesterone. The progesterone was tricky—he first had to use a thick needle and syringe to withdraw the drug from the bottle, then replace the thick needle with a thin one to inject me. One night he was shoving as hard as he could, but the needle would not go into my hip. I lay facedown on the bed, my tears trembling, feeling my skin ripped into, and then he realized his mistake. After a long day of work, his fatigue had caused him to forget to change the needles. He had been trying to shove the thick needle into my skin—the needle that was never meant to go into skin. Eventually we laughed about it. After one week of progesterone injections, I could hardly walk and felt like I had the flu. I phoned the doctor. He explained that a small percentage of women have a bad reaction to the injections, and I obviously was among that statistic. He gave me vaginal inserts instead.

My husband continued to inject me with Lupron each morning, and I continued the Estrace and progesterone. Five days before the procedure, I began taking Minocin and Medrol tablets several times a day—tricking my body more.

My older sister called the night before my scheduled IVF, I thought to wish me good luck. I answered all of her questions, but when she found out about the possible leftover embryos she said, "What a waste." It felt as though someone had thrown cold water on my body. Shaking and hurt I asked her, "What do you mean?"

"All those embryos—what a waste. I just think of what they could become."

I became defensive, a state of being that was becoming too common as I went through months and months of trying to get pregnant. "They're just cells. They're not babies."

"But they could be babies."

I closed the conversation. How could she do this to me? The last thing I needed was unnecessary stress before my IVF. I went to bed and meditated, but the relaxation seemed crowded by my thoughts of being too old. Was I not listening? Were my mother and sister right? Would I ruin my life by having a child that would be in high school when I'm in my fifties? And more importantly, would it be fair to my child? Was I making bad decisions?

My doctor's moral code was to insert only two embryos at a time. I lay on the gurney, my head in a surgery cap, my bladder full based on instruction, my husband standing close and holding my hand. The doctor inserted the catheter, then performed a test insemination with dye to be sure he was in the right spot. Then he inserted the embryos and I watched the tiny white spot rush into my womb. I beamed, the type of smile that hurts the cheeks.

Ten days later, after giving blood samples, my doctor phoned and told me I was pregnant with twins. The rush of excitement practically crushed my insides. An exemplary feeling that I had done it—with the help of others, but I had done it. I felt like a real woman, a maternal woman, a woman who had every right to have a baby, regardless of my age. I told friends and family, and I began looking at baby clothes. Six weeks into it, I bled. I went into the doctor's office and sat on the table as they watched the monitor displaying the uterine ultrasound. Nothing. No heartbeats; no embryos. They had vanished; my body had cleansed itself.

After I dressed, the doctor explained to me that, once again, I had fallen into a rare statistic. He said it was unusual for a woman to miscarry after IVF. The typical problem with IVF is that the embryos don't take. In an entire year, he had only had two patients who had miscarried after IVF: another woman and me. He told me to wait three months and then we would try again.

I felt humiliated having to explain to people that I was no longer pregnant. My aunt asked me why I had been gardening the day of the miscarriage, as though my pulling weeds had somehow caused the babies to dislodge. I felt sad as two of my friends gave birth to their healthy babies. I had nothing but happiness for them, but for me, I felt almost detached from my own body. Whose body was this? This old body that could not keep embryos in place. This wise body that knew we had been trying to trick it.

Yet I bounced back; I knew it did me no good to dwell. We tried again. The same drugs, the same procedures, everything the same, and the same wonderful results: pregnant with twins. With the doctor's approval, we went on vacation. We stayed in a beach house in South Carolina with my extended family, and I went in twice to a local clinic to have my blood drawn and sent back to Colorado to monitor my progress. Again, I beamed. This time, I told only one close friend, my mother, and my sisters. We lounged on the beach, ate excellent food, watched the gray pelicans fly back and forth each morning and evening. But I felt as though something was wrong, incomplete. I called the doctor for the latest news on my blood tests, and he told me that I had lost one. My husband and I sat on the bed in the beach house, watching the massive sea, still clinging to that one embryo, hoping that it would cling to me. We flew home.

Six weeks into it, I felt cramping. I went to the bathroom and saw the blood. And this time, I saw the embryo. I stared into the water with so much disbelief I had to call my husband to come look.

"Is it what I think it is?"

"Yes," he said. He walked me out of the bathroom, wrapped his arms around me, and we cried.

Once again my doctor admitted his disbelief. "One miscarriage was odd; two miscarriages with IVF is incredibly rare." He told me again to wait three months. In those months, a cyst developed on my right ovary: a normal cyst, a cyclic cyst, expected to go away like most do. But it didn't. It stayed and remained the same size. My doctor finally ordered a laparoscopy. I went into surgery, and he found the cyst was in actuality a tumor. When I woke and he told me, I tensed and immediately thought of cancer. After losing three friends in the previous five years to cancer, I wondered if I had done this to myself. If my determination had clouded my actual abilities. If I had asked too much of my aging body.

With the second laparoscopy, my doctor removed the tumor along with my right ovary and right fallopian tube. He did not want to take any chances by disrupting a tumor that was possibly malignant. As I laid at home recovering from surgery, wondering if I had cancer, I realized that even if I never became pregnant, by going through all of this, the tumor had been found and removed. That in itself would be enough.

The call came a few days later. Benign. Let's heal, let's get on with it, let's do this thing. My mother suddenly flipped her attitude. She began to support me, encourage me, fill me with such kind words that I forgot my age, forgot my losses, finally felt that it was OK to be my age and try to have a baby.

We had three embryos left. Four had previously been implanted and one did not thaw correctly, so it had been discarded. We waited three months. This time, my doctor put me on a blood thinner call Lovenox to try to prevent a third miscarriage. And this time, I gave myself the injections. I thought it was ridiculous that after all I had been through I could not give myself a shot. So each morning I injected myself with Lupron, and I injected myself with Lovenox. Two injections a day for one month. My stomach became black and blue. The skin had grown thick where the needles went in, so each morning I had to navigate the bruises and find a tender spot that would accept the needle once more.

The night before my last IVF, my husband and I sat at the kitchen table. We had been trying for two years solid. My body had been through drugs, hormones, injections, two surgeries, two miscarriages. He said if this one didn't work, we could move to adoption. But I was spent. I had had my fill of disappointment. I apologized to him and explained that I was done.

The doctor thawed all three embryos, yet only two were acceptable. He performed the IVF, and I saw the white dot. I meditated, I relaxed, and I focused on work. Ten days later, the doctor called to tell me that I was pregnant with one—the other embryo hadn't taken. I remained calm. The excitement was different this time, more serene. I had never felt healthier in my life, and I stayed focused on this one last embryo inside of me. Six weeks into it, I went in for an ultrasound, and there it was. A heartbeat. One lone heartbeat, one tiny being existing in my body. I had to continue to give myself daily injections of the blood thinner through my entire first trimester. As my belly began to grow, the black and blue bruises stretched. I felt nauseated and fatigued, but I never threw up and I managed to eat and to work each day. Every evening I collapsed on the bed and watched bad TV.

After the first trimester, I felt remarkable. I did yoga each morning and walked the dogs before I began my workday telecommuting from home. I talked to the baby inside of me; I read to it. My husband and I decided to wait to know the gender so I began calling the baby my Honeybee. I decorated the nursery and bought baby clothes. My family and friends threw me a baby shower. The feeling of growing a human being inside of me moved me into another frame of mind—a bigger connectedness, a stability in my senses. And I soon realized this baby was definitely a part of me. It had come from a stranger's egg, but it was biologically mine. My forty-three-year-old body was doing just fine developing a life-form.

Toward the end of the third trimester, my husband and I hired a doula and learned hypnobirthing techniques. I went into labor two weeks early and was six centimeters by the time I arrived at the hospital. We thought the baby would be there in no time, but of course, like everything else, I would have to work for it. Our hospital room was exactly as I had asked for. Quiet, as few disturbances as possible, a bath to relax in, my own soothing music. The room was warm and comfortable and swollen with the tenderness of my husband. I labored for nineteen hours with no pain meds, three of those on Pitocin, a drug used to induce delivery—a drug that increases the pain of contractions. Finally, in the dark, hushed room, with no one but my husband, our doula, the midwife, and the nurse, they told me the baby who was sunny-side up was not coming. It could not get past my pelvic bone. They called in a doctor and he explained that he understood I was adamant about avoiding a cesarean section. Because the baby was not in distress, he agreed to let me push for a while. I had an epidural, got some rest, and drank some chicken broth. I pushed for three hours with a fever; still the baby remained calm and would not come out. They wheeled me in for the cesarean.

In our birth plan, my husband and I had written that we wanted the gender to be announced to me by my husband. We had chosen a girl's name and a boy's name. The C-section was simple; the baby had not gone far so was easily scooped out of my womb. I heard the cries, which made me cry. I couldn't see the baby. I stared at the fluorescent lights and listened to the scuttle in the background, listened to my baby. My husband leaned down and quietly said in my ear, "Penny wants to meet you." He laid her on top of my chest. Our Penny. Bundled calmly on top of me, her eyes struggling to find her way into the brightness. My husband and I silently cried.

I am forty-seven now, and my daughter is three and a half. Many of the friends I grew up with are now grandmothers. I feel young. I run around with Penny, play games with her, keep up with the young moms. It does not matter where she came from or how old I am. She is bonded to me, and I to her. When she is old enough, I will tell her about a wonderful stranger who helped me bring her into this world. But she will understand that my blood flowed through her. I fed her in the womb, breastfed her through her first year, made all of her baby food from scratch, and now, I will guide her like a mother does. And if she someday feels embarrassed because her mother is old, I will help her understand how determination has nothing to do with age. I will help her know that I made the right decision.

Alisa A. Gaston-Linn's work has appeared in *The Sun*, *The Montreal Review*, *Hawaii Pacific Review*, *Fiction 365*, *The Faircloth Review*, *Rocky Mountain Parent*, *Black Hearts* magazine, and other publications. She received her master's in liberal studies with advanced study in creative writing from the University of Denver, spent several years as a technical/web writer and editor for the US Antarctic Program, and has taught creative writing to youth at Lighthouse Writers in Denver. She has also volunteered as a creative writing facilitator for the Boys and Girls Club and Urban Peak Teen Shelter. She is currently working on a novel.

Story Reflection Questions

1. What is one moment in the story that stayed with you?

   _____

   _____

   _____

2. What questions did you find yourself asking as you read the story?

   _____

   _____

   _____

3. What challenged you about the story?

   _____

   _____

   _____

4. What surprised you about the story?

   _____

   _____

   _____

5. How does this story relate to your own life experience?

   _____

   _____

   _____

Trying

Desaray Smith

Try #1

I'm in California on my honeymoon. I'm on the BART. My wife has a vial of sperm tucked inside the breast pocket of her down jacket. It's like we found a baby bird.

Try #4

We are back home in North Carolina. We've been together almost four years. We are using frozen sperm from a small sperm bank. Our donor is gay. He writes on his profile that he is into Buddhism and has a deaf brother. I want to ask a friend for sperm, but my wife doesn't trust a "real" person. Plus, the guy we asked said no because he didn't want to be like his father who left.

The nurse who runs the sperm bank is gay and Jewish. His husband writes prescriptions for medical marijuana out of the same office, which is basically the basement of their house. The bank lets gay men donate, and older men, which isn't against the law, but it's not recommended. The nurse is a sperm-bank renegade. He believes it's not your sexual orientation or age that makes a baby. Love makes a baby—and well-rounded sperm with strong tails. He is one of my people.

The other reason I picked this bank is that we can meet the donor almost right away. The baby doesn't have to wait until she is eighteen to find out who her donor is. When she is born, they will give me the donor's name and number. We could all go out to lunch before the belly button thingy even falls off. Also, this sperm bank is cheaper than any other sperm bank. Sperm for people, not profit.

Try #5

My wife and I give up on at-home inseminations and go to a fertility clinic for procedures and shots and pills. The fertility clinic tells us this sperm sample is bad. Maybe it's just a fluke. The renegade nurse gives us the next month for free. That sperm sample is bad too. Maybe the samples have been bad the whole time, but maybe they haven't. We run out of money and take a break; six months later, my wife leaves me for another woman. I don't think one thing has anything to do with the other. They just happened back to back.

Break #1

Right after my wife leaves, a coworker offers me her husband's sperm. I have no idea why she's offering me her husband's sperm or why her husband says yes. I notice that all of her white friends come from rough backgrounds or are gay. She knows I've never met my mom and my dad was a drug addict. I was in foster care once too. Why, I've even spent the night in a domestic violence shelter. I feel like these things give me some kind of credibility. Like, the black and brown people in my life find out these things and think, "Surely this is the kind of white lady who won't touch my hair." But also, I have big hips and say true things and funny things, sometimes loudly. Or maybe it's because I can say the word "black" without stuttering and looking away. I let people finish their sentences. Sometimes, when I really think about it, though, I don't understand why any of my black friends are friends with me. I certainly don't run around trying to make friends with men and straight people. So maybe that's it. I tend to go for people who are braver and nicer than I am. On bad days, though, I have a hard time understanding why we try to make friends with anyone. We all just end up moving away.

Anyway, I say yes to the sperm.

Try #7

I've been single for nine months. For my thirty-fourth birthday, I make myself a cake. I light my own candles and blow them out alone. I put my dog in the car and drive two hours to Charlotte. My coworker's husband hands me his sperm, and I drive off. I park in front of some kind of warehouse. I inseminate myself in the front seat with my butt propped up on the steering wheel. I'm looking up at the stars and listening to good music. I fall back in love with my life. It really is that romantic. My life and I are on a new adventure.

I get pregnant. I make an appointment with the local midwives. The day I decide on names, the miscarriage starts. I call the midwives. One of them says, "Maybe it's implantation bleeding."

The next morning, I go to the bathroom and feel it fall out of me. Before I know it, I'm on my knees, pawing through the bloody pee. But, at this point, how could I tell the difference between toilet paper and a baby? I go back to bed. I go to my appointment. The midwife is old and brusque and has short hair. I wonder if she is gay. I tell her I am. She recommends a sonogram to confirm the miscarriage and then a D&C to get the rest of it. I refuse. The midwife suggests that I can't be her client if I don't take her recommendations. I tell her she just has to document that I said no. She says, "Are you a nurse?"

I say, "Social worker."

At some point, the midwife turns to me and says, "Did you even want this pregnancy?" She says it like queers get pregnant by accident and then have to decide whether or not they want it. I'm hurt, but at least now I know she's not gay.

Break # 2

I am in love with a new girl. We've been dating for three months. She has lots of tattoos; she buys me gorgeous flowers. Like, not carnations. She has the slyest sense of humor. She is a medical student, and her mother is a poet. She told me she didn't always want kids, but then she did her pediatrics rotation. She probably had her heart broken and put back together so many times it started to look like a mother's heart. Or maybe a father's. I haven't asked her which one.

I've been going to this support group for women who are interested in birth. It's called a holistic birth collective. Some of the women are pregnant; some are trying; some women have ten-year-olds. It's run by a midwife who delivers babies at home. Where I live, it's illegal to help someone give birth at home. The meetings are about astral planes and natural birth and how to make vitamins and art out of your placenta. I don't believe in half of this stuff, but every week I walk out of those meetings feeling like I could actually get pregnant someday. I decide I'm ready to try again. I call my coworker. She tells me she and her husband are divorcing. I call her husband; he says he won't be available. I call my high school sweetheart in New York. He says yes and buys a ticket.

Try #8

The medical student helps deliver her first baby. She texts me right after. Later, I ask her to inseminate me. She says yes. She brings a plastic speculum and a headlamp. She is nervous and earnest and so impossibly excited. After two divorces and a miscarriage, I lay back and look at her. I'm grateful to be reminded of what it feels like to be nervous and earnest and impossibly excited. She has stars tattooed on her shoulders.

Break #3

Sometimes the medical student withdraws into this icy, silent place and I can't get her out. Left to my own devices, I make long lists of all the reasons she's going to be a bad wife and mother. I break up with her. I break up with trying. Except that I get a part-time job working seven days a week so I can start saving up for the next round of tries. There's this one girl I'm dating, she has the word *Daddy* tattooed on her chest. A few years ago, one of her exes got pregnant and had a baby right after they broke up. She calls him her son; sometimes he treats her like a dad. They look exactly alike. She is tall and lithe, and when we have sex, I feel like a real woman, like the kind that has sex with men and gets pregnant. I think of her as a conception doula.

I go on a spiritual retreat about letting go of the past. I decide to buy a house. It has two bedrooms—one for me and one for the baby. I ask the builders to finish the basement. Maybe I could trade child care for a room. Everybody in this town barters for everything. I decide to try again. I call my donor. He says he might be going to China. He applied for a program. The girl I'm dating breaks up with me. She is polyamorous and our relationship isn't good for her primary partner. I book a flight to New York.

Try #11

My donor lives with his very elderly great-grandmother, who raised him. I inseminate in his childhood bedroom while he plays video games in the living room. He's really into video games. He's wearing a headset. He looks like Janet Jackson during the Rhythm Nation tour.

Try #12

My donor is diagnosed with thyroid cancer. He says he wants to keep trying anyway. He has never met his mother either. I fly to New York for an insemination. We are in an Irish bar in Flushing. Ginuwine is on the jukebox. I can't help but look at the tumor. I say something. He looks over my shoulder at his reflection in the mirror. He can see it too. He moves it around with his fingers. "Wow. I didn't realize it was so big."

Try #13

I start going to a new clinic. I have a consultation with the doctor. "Will you do inseminations for an unmarried couple?" Since we are not actually a couple, this question is awkward, but I don't know how else to put it. The doctor says yes, but he has to find some special paperwork. I go through all the same tests I went through last time. I'm still normal. His nurse knows my donor is flying in. "When will Jamar be here?" I decide I like her.

The next day, I pick Jamar up from the airport and the transmission falls out of my car. I take a taxi to the clinic. I forget the special paperwork. They say they can't do the insemination without it. "If I had walked in here with a ring on my finger, you wouldn't have batted an eyelash. Straight people just tell you they are married and you believe it. No special paperwork for them."

I take another taxi home, have Jamar sign the special paperwork, and take a taxi back. I get inseminated. I lay alone in a dark room for thirty minutes with my hips propped up on a disposable pillow. Nobody comes to tell me the time's up, but I figure it is. I get dressed. I poke my head into someone's office. A woman says, "Oh, we forgot about you."

Try #16

My donor is cancer free. He got into the program. This is the last try. I tell myself this has to be it. "I'm done." Besides, I'm white and always sad. My black child will hate herself, if she makes it out of the lake I drive us into. Remember that lady who drove her children into the lake? Nikki Giovanni wrote a poem about her. I've always identified with her. I'm not fit to be a mother. I get inseminated. I lay in a dark room for thirty minutes with my hips propped up on a disposable pillow. Some nurse comes in. "I guess we will let you out now," she says and laughs, like being in jail is funny, like comparing this to jail is funny.

Break #4

I'm not pregnant for the last time. The fourth anniversary of my first try comes and goes. Maybe I'll move to California. My best friend lives there. I go to her baby shower. I drink mimosas. She tells me about a clinic that will put somebody else's embryo in you, like somebody else's egg and somebody else's sperm. I literally can't understand what she is saying as a concept. "It's an adoption from conception," she says. "You get three tries for ten thousand dollars."

I keep dating. One girl wants to be monogamous after three weeks. I say no. Within the month, her new girlfriend, who is still married and has two kids, moves in. The next girl tells me that she doesn't think gay people should have babies because we are nature's birth control. I am so appalled, I feel like I'm having an out-of-body experience. The next girl says she loves me, but I never say it back. She starts buying kid-sized rocking chairs. She breaks up with me. She burns the chairs and posts a picture of the bonfire on her blog. The next girl is a boy. "I'm not, like, a *dude* dude," he says. He wanted to be the one to have the baby. He bought a house with a second bedroom. I've never dated someone who wanted this like I do. It makes me feel a different kind of sad.

I stop dating for a month. I make a new friend. She is gay and single. She has tried too: doctors, miscarriages, debt. She is on the other side of trying, but I'm not. I'm drinking beer and crying, telling her my little story. Every time I talk about not having a baby, I cry. I say, "Maybe I could try again. Maybe if I just do IVF, I can be done with it." I'm still working a lot. I see a woman in the emergency room who needs detox. She is pregnant. I ask how she is paying for drugs. She doesn't really answer. I say, "Some women in your situation exchange sex for drugs or money. Is that true for you?" She says yes. She cries. I tell her it's OK and mean it.

I can't stop thinking about the medical student. I send her a Facebook message. We go out. She is wearing that leather jacket I love. I say, "I'm going to move to California next year." I tell her maybe I'll try IVF in California. Then I joke that I'll have to move into my mother's basement if it works.

She says, "Why not try IVF here?" She says it doesn't make sense to move to California, get pregnant, and then have to move again. She tells me about this doctor she knows. She trips over the word "we" more than once. "You," she says. "You could go to him."

She tells me she doesn't give people the silent treatment anymore. I tell her about this self-help book I've been meaning to read. "Maybe it will explain why I feel so far away all of the time." I walk her home. I kiss her forehead. Then her cheek and her neck, then her temple and her jaw, but not her lips. I breathe in her hair and the collar of her jacket. I breathe out whiskey. I say good-night.

———

Desaray Smith is a thirty-six-year-old queer femme, Quaker, and social worker living in Asheville, North Carolina, by way of Washington, DC; Miami, Florida; Oakland, California; and a few other places it pains her to mention. If you would like to know more about letting go and letting God, feminism, white people, the art of the promise, the pitfalls of sarcasm, lesbian baby-making, staying in touch, the North, the South, forgiveness, BDSM, how to rollover a 403b, or how to pack and then unpack a box, she can be reached at desarayhelensmith@gmail.com.

Story Reflection Questions

1. What is one moment in the story that stayed with you?

   _____
   _____
   _____

2. What questions did you find yourself asking as you read the story?

   _____
   _____
   _____

3. What challenged you about the story?

   _____
   _____
   _____

4. What surprised you about the story?

   _____
   _____
   _____

5. How does this story relate to your own life experience?

   _____
   _____
   _____

Nasaan ka anak ko?
A Queer Filipina American
Feminist's Tale of Abortion
and Self-Recovery

Patricia Justine Tumang

Jamila May Joseph is the name of my biracial daughter who was never born. She has dark brown crescent half-moons for eyes and a fiery tongue like her mother. Her skin is the color of the midnight sky, like her black Kenyan father. Her spirit talks to me in waking dreams. She crawls toward me on the knotted rug and smiles briefly, exposing two white knobs for teeth. I see her grow up. She learns how to walk and utters her first words. Whispering "mama" into my ears, she rejoices in love, forgiving me again and again. Sometimes I stop seeing her, a blank space of clarity replacing memories unmade. I look in the corners and underneath the pillows. I call her name but only hear the faint rustling of wind. I remember then that she is dead, a bloody mass of tissue flushed down the toilet. The abortion was an act of desperation. The malicious guilt never brings her back. *Nasaan ka anak ko?* Where are you, my daughter?

The name Jamila means "beautiful" in Arabic. During my senior year of college, I studied abroad in Kenya for five months. While learning about Islam, Swahili civilization, and Kenyan culture, I discovered I was pregnant. George, my lover, was a Methodist black Kenyan—a rarity for the predominantly Muslim population on the Kenyan coast. I met him at a small guesthouse in Lamu where he worked as the houseboy.

When I returned to New York City after the program ended, I was nearly two months pregnant and had no financial means to support a child. My first intention was to keep it, so I told my middle-class Filipino mother about my pregnancy and she threatened to withdraw her financial support. I was in a bind—emotionally, spiritually, and financially. I was in a spiritual turmoil, not because of my parents' Catholic beliefs, but rather because I felt connected to the baby's spirit. But I could not envision myself giving up the middle-class privileges I grew up with to become a single mother who works two jobs while finishing school.

My mother and I fought about it constantly. She wanted me to finish my education and not be burdened with the responsibilities of raising a child at my age. I couldn't believe that my devoutly Catholic Filipino mother was urging me to have an abortion. Several months after the abortion, my mother revealed to me that she was pro-choice. She equated the idea of pro-choice with pro-abortion, but I understood what she was really saying. I was not in a position to have the baby.

My mother never spoke to me about sexuality when I was a little girl, let alone the topic of abortion, and it was assumed I was heterosexual. At age twenty-one, I came out to her as bisexual, and she immediately dismissed me. "What do you mean," she said, "that you are bisexual and that you are attracted to women? That's not natural!" Because she perceived heterosexuality as inherent to my sexuality, she never lost hope that someday I would meet the perfect man and reproduce for our namesake. But a poor black man from Kenya was not what she had in mind.

When I got my first period at the age of eleven, no one talked to me about my body and its development. Instead, my family made jokes about the female children and their impending womanhood. Tita Leti, my father's cousin, would embarrass me and my cousins at Christmas by giving us gift-wrapped boxes of little girls' underwear. Decorated with kittens or puppies on pink or yellow cotton, my cousin Vinci and I dreaded the thought of wearing them. Periods, we reasoned, were a sign that we were women. Tita Leti said to our parents, "Now you have to watch out and make sure they close their legs like good girls!" We cringed at their laughter, yet it was only in these jokes that sexuality, in heterosexual terms, was ever hinted at.

I learned about sexual development from school textbooks and discussed it with my high school female friends, all of whom were Filipino and straight. We talked about heterosexual sex and had unprotected sex with men. Many of my friends became pregnant and had abortions, though they didn't speak about it. They were perfect Asian girls—they couldn't. They acted calm, collected, and recovered. Until I experienced it myself, I didn't realize how much the silence burned my insides and that I, too, was in denial about my situation: having an abortion that I didn't want and experiencing physical trauma resulting from complications with the abortion.

My own model minority expectations influenced my decision to have an abortion. I wasn't sure I could cope with my family and society's prejudices against my half-black child. To me, being the model minority daughter meant assimilating, speaking perfect English, adhering to a middle-class lifestyle, and establishing a successful career after college. Not being heterosexual, having a biracial baby, and being a single mother were not a part of these expectations. Having internalized my parents' expectations and the United States' views on what a model minority is, I felt even more pressure to have an abortion. Not having any financial help from my mother pushed me to my final decision. I took the RU-486 pill and hoped the worst would be over.

For the next couple of weeks I endured a living nightmare. The first dosage of Mifeprex, a medication that blocks a hormone needed for a pregnancy to continue, was given to me in pill form at the clinic. When I got home, I inserted four tablets of Misoprostol vaginally. These two medications combined to terminate the pregnancy nonsurgically. Heavy bleeding for up to two weeks was expected.

I didn't realize the horrible truth of that statement until I lay awake at night in fits of unbearable pain, bleeding through sanitary napkins by the hour. When I was in the bathroom one night, clumps of bloody tissue and embryonic remains fell into the toilet. I was overcome with tremors, my body shaking with a burst of feverish heat. My cheeks flushed as sweat bled into my hairline. Dragging my feet on the cold tiled floor, I went back to bed and hid under the covers. Eyes open and bloodshot, knees to my chest, I cried until I fell asleep.

Returning to the clinic several days later for a scheduled follow-up, I learned that the gestational sac was still intact. I was given another dose of Mifeprex and Misoprostol. That night, I stared in horror as a clump of tissue the size of a baseball escaped from my body. I held this bloody mass in my hand, feeling the watery red liquid drip from my fingers. The tissue was soft and pliable. Poking at the flesh, I imagined the life that it embodied. The sac looked like a bleeding pig's heart. For several months after, the sight of blood made me vomit.

As I was going through this experience, I remembered from my childhood the subtitled Asian movies that featured abortion scenes. In these films, Asian women drank exotic herbal concoctions to terminate their pregnancies and then jumped up and down on the stairs. Scenes showed their mothers holding their hands while their fetuses became detached. In one scene, a desperate woman took a hanger and mutilated her body, plunging rusty wires into her uterus. *Did that really happen?* I wondered. *Where were those young Asian women bleeding to death? Were they real? Were they alive? How did they heal from such a trauma?* Watching these images, I wondered if I could heal from my experience. Was I alone?

Deciding to have an abortion was the hardest decision I have ever made. I made it alone. Without my mother's support and in George's absence, I felt I couldn't have a child. George was very supportive despite his pro-life Christian views. Communicating through sporadic e-mail messages and long-distance telephone calls, he said he valued my safety and saw the reality of our situation. For a moment, however, I imagined what it would be like if I could marry my poor Kenyan lover and bring him to the United States to be a family. The "American Dream." George would work at a deli or be the security guard on campus while I finished college and attained a bachelor's degree in cultural studies with a path in race, ethnicity, and postcolonialism. I would engage him in a postmodern discourse on the white supremacist patriarchy of America and the productions of multiculturalism in the media and art, while he brought home his minimum-wage salary. Our daughter would live in a world that would exoticize and tokenize her for her kinky hair, brown skin, Asian eyes, and multilingual tongue. What does it mean that I had the capability of giving birth to new possibilities but chose to bleed her away?

I thought of my mother: a young, vibrant, and hopeful Filipina immigrant who came to America decades ago, determined to make a decent living in the land of "equal opportunity." She was twenty-two years old when she gave birth to me. I was twenty-two and bleeding away. Feeling utterly dehumanized, my body an unrecognizable grotesque monster spitting out blood, I wondered about the possibility of spiritual rebirth from experiences of trauma and dehumanization. I thought of loss and survival and what this means for many of us raised among immigrant families from "developing" countries. I thought of my parents' transition from working class to middle class and remembered clearly the losses we paid for while assimilating into a racist culture. Society gave us capital for becoming model minorities yet systematically berated us because of our differences. We lost our mother tongue and shed our rich cultural histories as we ate hamburgers and spoke English like "true Americans."

During this time I longed to read the writings of women of color for inspiration. I scanned the libraries and searched online for feminist narratives written by women of color on abortion and found none. A majority of the books documented the political history of abortion as it impacts the lives of white women. A friend suggested I read Alice Walker's *In Search of Our Mother's Gardens*. Choking on tears, I read about Walker's abortion in the mid-1960s when she returned to the United States from a trip to Africa. She had been a senior in college and discovered that she was pregnant, alone, and penniless. Thinking of Walker's time, when safe and legal abortions were a privilege, I counted my blessings and buried my pain in the depths of me, far from eyes that see, in a solitary place where whispers mingle and collide in silence.

In the culture of silence that was pervasive in my Filipino household, children—particularly little girls—were not allowed to speak unless spoken to. I learned at an early age the art of keeping silent. I knew to keep quiet when my father's expression became stern and a hardened thin line formed on his forehead. All the pains, joys, and heartaches of my life festered inside me, creating gaping wounds between the silences. My tongue was a well, containing words fit to burst and flood the Pacific Ocean. Yet only English came out. In short. And polite. Sentences. At home and abroad we sang in English, raged in English, loved and dreamed in English.

As a child I found inexplicable joy in singing Tagalog songs that I had learned by listening to my parents' Filipino audiotapes given to us by visiting relatives. They were played only on special occasions. Although I couldn't understand a word, I sang unabashedly. The act of singing in Tagalog was dangerous and daring. Rooted in a desperate aching to speak a language other than English, I felt like a mischievous child stealing a cookie from the forbidden cookie jar, and I slowly savored every bite. In this hunger, I realized the power of voice even while I couldn't speak. Later I realized that writing was another way to emerge from the silence into a place of healing.

I looked to writing as a means for what black feminist writer bell hooks has termed "self-recovery." I wrote for survival about the physical and emotional abuse I experienced as a child in a sexist household. And later I wrote to recover from my traumatic abortion. I found strength in the words of Alice Walker, Cherríe Moraga, Nellie Wong, Audre Lorde, Lois-Ann Yamanaka, Gloria Anzaldúa, Maxine Hong Kingston, Angela Davis, and Mitsuye Yamada. I read until my vision was a blur. The battles and writings of these women inspired me to heal. I, too, wanted to break the silence that oppressed me.

When considering abortion options, my friends in New York had encouraged me to take RU-486. They told me it would be an easier experience than a surgical abortion. Finding information on the pill wasn't difficult. It was introduced to the American market in September 2000 but had been available in Europe for many years. I conducted online research and realized I had to make a quick decision. It was only prescribed to women who were less than seven weeks pregnant, and I was a budding eight weeks then. RU-486 appealed to me because it had an efficiency rate of 99 percent and was nonsurgical. I contacted a small primary health-care clinic in Brooklyn that offered the pill for women up to nine weeks pregnant. It was the same price as a surgical abortion and was advertised as being "less traumatic." According to my research, RU-486 was given commendable reviews by women who had tried it.

If I had known how traumatic my experience with RU-486 would be, I would have opted for the surgical method. Not that it would have been less traumatic, but anything would have been better than the three weeks of horrendous hemorrhaging and cramping I endured. My friends' support helped me through the difficult moments, but those who had urged me to take the pill had known nothing about it, nor had they any personal experience with it. Those who had had surgical abortions just thought the pill would be "easier" by comparison. The doctor who had prescribed me the pill told me that although she had never taken it, she had heard that the procedure was only slightly uncomfortable. I had no adequate aftercare or education about the side effects, except what was written in small print on the pamphlets I was given. My doctor had informed me that all the information I needed to know was right there. I felt so terrifyingly alone in the process.

Healing eventually came from actively talking about my abortion with my mother and friends. Whether through speech or writing, it meant consciously remembering the experience. It meant talking about how our bodies have never been our own. It meant finding strength in the words of other women of color to contextualize and validate my experience as a queer Asian American woman having to contend with predominantly white narratives regarding reproductive rights and abortion access and experiences. Even for those who can afford to get an abortion, in my experience there has been a serious lack of education about procedures and proper emotional and physical aftercare. While many women have had positive experiences with RU-486, mine was not. Almost a year after the abortion, the emotional and spiritual pain still visited me from time to time. For so long I tried to deny that I had undergone a traumatic experience, and I entered a period of self-punishment. I pretended to be recovered, but the pain pushed itself outward. Regret and guilt caused severe anxiety attacks that left me breathless, convulsing, and faint.

When I returned to the clinic after the abortion, I was told I needed therapy for my depression and anxiety. A white female doctor began asking questions about me, my family, and my refusal to seek therapy. I suggested joining a support group for women of color who had had abortions, but the doctor informed me that there were none, to her knowledge, in New York City. She asked me why I would feel more comfortable around other women of color and not a white man. I felt extremely uncomfortable with her questioning, and she pressed on, a few words short of calling me a "separatist." Since my own abortion, I have realized that women of color need access to postabortion therapy that is affordable, accessible, and sensitive to different cultures and sexualities.

To fully heal, I ultimately have had to let go. I didn't let go of the memory but of this imaginary noose that restrained me and kept me from self-love. I hadn't learned as a child to love myself. Rather, I had been taught to be a good Filipina girl and do as I was told. This noose now came in forms of denial, self-punishment, and attracting unsupportive people. I also had to take some time away from my mother, to retreat from her anger and hurt to process my own. The first few months after the abortion, we didn't speak that often. Eventually I entered therapy, which my mother paid for out of guilt, despite our emotional distance. Talking about my abortion with another woman of color proved a relief. I found support and a safe space to open up.

My mother eventually broke down. She missed me and was worried about me. She apologized for not supporting me during my ordeal. I knew in my heart that if I was to forgive myself, I must also forgive her. She too was wounded and realized that she would not have known what to do in my situation. I felt closer to her at that point.

Healing has never been an easy process for me. Something always interrupts it: new relationships, disagreements with family or friends, old issues, work, or school. Denial coats the pain and prevents actual healing. When I become scared of my emotions and feel buried, I remember to love myself and know that I am not alone. I struggle with my inner demons constantly. Although I am only in the beginning stages of my healing process, I feel that I have now entered a place of peace. Regret does nothing to change things. Although my decision was difficult, I made the best choice for my circumstances.

It is my daughter's spirit that calls me out of grief. In my insistence on remembering her, I have found healing. She comes to me in dreams and comforts me during difficult times. She gives me a vision for the future where there is love instead of suffering, a place where there is healing from dehumanization. I struggle for her vision every day.

Nasaan ka anak ko?

Patricia Justine is a writer whose recent work focuses on contemporary art in the Philippines. In 2012 she received a grant from the Creative Capital Warhol Foundation to write about contemporary Filipina artists and was awarded a Fulbright Fellowship in 2009 to conduct research on historical representations of women during the Philippine Revolution. Now based in Manila, Tumang previously resided in Oakland, California, where she earned an MFA in English and creative writing from Mills College in 2006 and received a Hedgebrook Residency for Women Authoring Change in 2007. She is coeditor of the anthology entitled *Homelands: Women's Journeys Across Race, Place, and Time* (Seal Press, 2006). In 2002 she earned her BA in cultural studies with a path in race, ethnicity, and postcolonialism from Eugene Lang College in New York City. Her work has appeared in *Colonize This! Young Women of Color on Today's Feminism* (Seal Press, 2002).

Story Reflection Questions

1. What is one moment in the story that stayed with you?

    _____

    _____

    _____

2. What questions did you find yourself asking as you read the story?

    _____

    _____

    _____

3. What challenged you about the story?

    _____

    _____

    _____

4. What surprised you about the story?

    _____

    _____

    _____

5. How does this story relate to your own life experience?

    _____

    _____

    _____

Letter to the Parent of My Child

Moki Macías

Loving you is easy. It's the wide-open-hearted, steady, delighting love that I'm made for. I always secretly judged the people I knew who were afraid of loving, who needed a warm-up period or some convincing. But then I began loving you and intertwining my life in yours and became obsessed with your death. What if you were gone, from one moment to another? Jeannette Winterson's opening line of a novel surfacing in my head—why is the measure of love loss? The measure of my love is how afraid I am of you not existing. Not of falling out of love, of you leaving me or me leaving you, but you not existing. This was my warm-up.

When I got pregnant, we did the insemination and right after I had to fly to Miami, waiting for my temperature to rise in my hotel room. I walked on the beach the night it did, and it was December and the wind, like the waves, was rolling and frothy with sand. I imagine it now all intermingled, the neon lights and the thick warm air and some small universe inside me expanding, breaking into new constellations.

On the rainy night we found out, after the initial excitement and phone calls and grinning at each other for an hour over bowls of pho, our fingers smelling of basil and lime, the thing that welled up in me was an emotion I've always entertained quite casually. I felt vulnerable. Vulnerable in the way that I do when you leave the house and I let myself think—just quickly, a bad habit like biting off a jagged nail—about all the things that could happen to you out there. I felt taken over; I felt superstitious; I felt obsessed with a tiny speck of neon sand, containing constellations within it.

I was tensing myself for loss. Sure of it when at five weeks pregnant we both got the flu and couldn't move for days, and K came over and bathed me in wet towels, trying to get my fever down. Looking for blood every time I sat on the toilet. You were so happy, and I felt like I needed some wooing, like I wasn't sure I should let my guard down for this stranger inside of me.

Before we got pregnant, we talked so much about how people would interact with our family, what it would feel like for us to walk out into the world every day, when our child would start noticing how the world responds to us, and what they will feel about it—our mixedness, our queerness. When what we experience individually or together now—experiences that we have intellectual weapons against, for which we have life preservers of humor, irony, and anger to buoy us—tilts full force against this new little person, unsuspecting. How will our child be racialized? How will our child make sense of their own identity? How will our child possibly find their people? As the (more) white parent, I have been amazed at how easily friends or acquaintances expect that my role in helping our child navigate the morass of race in the United States will be to get out of the way as much as possible. They expect that I will earnestly take on imparting the cultural markers and ethnic traditions of your ancestral people (ones that you may or may not have access to yourself, being raised mixed in the United States). While they might have felt discomfited if I were to do this as a way of interacting with you—cheerfully appropriating a culture not my own as a way to close the gap of experience between us—somehow it is expected as a white parent to a child of color. They expect, rightly, that the world will read our child as a person of color, like you are read as a person of color, and that the best gift to our child is a strong ethnic identity that affirms this. But must both of us hide parts of ourselves to do this?

I think about how we have both come to understand mixedness in our own lives, about how we have both carried continents—and the great span of distance between them—under our skin. Our mothers both immigrants to the United States, those mother tongues denied us. The way we came to understand race through the prism of our own families, black and Asian and Latino and white, and when we began to recognize the cultures of our people that had absorbed into our own being—Korean and Austrian and Chicano and Southern white.

To claim my mixedness is not a way out of whiteness or the protections it inevitably offers me. But my treason to white supremacy is to understand the experience of whiteness as both violence reaped and deep loss. White supremacy asks that I would not only reject my father's name, but my mother's Austrian food, values, and traditions. Whiteness that leaves one peopleless, the wind whistling through one's skin.

I imagine our mixed baby describing who they are. Will they say what you say? Will they say mixed? Will they say Korean American? Will they say Southern or American (like you do to stop the conversation when the person asking doesn't deserve a response)? Most likely, whiteness won't ever protect our child or give them any privileges. But I have more to offer our child than thin, transparent places of loss that let the wind through, or power wielded over others. Doesn't our child deserve my people's food? My people's values and ceremonies? Doesn't our child deserve to feel their mixedness as something of value? We are lucky, in that way. Having our two old-world mothers around to speak this sense of mixedness into existence, their thick accents and their food and their competing ideas of modernity. Having the blood and chosen families that we do.

At six months pregnant, the baby is real now—real enough to feel through my skin, to kick you at night when I sleep up against you. As soon as I started to show, my belly getting taut, breasts heavy, the straight world wanted so much to claim me. More than ever before, my body became a confirmation of my already assumed straightness, and the clue to your gender. When we are together there is much less hesitation, sir, when addressing you. I wonder if this will happen when the baby gets here—our child gendering us less queer. Even when they know we are queer—the people we work with, casual acquaintances—there is an assumed camaraderie around child-rearing that makes me uncomfortable. Like our queer lives have suddenly become less foreign to them, like we just happen to be gay, but queer culture and queer community and queer politics don't exist. The man you worked with who, when you shared our decision not to learn what sex the ultrasound technician would have assigned, said, "But how will you know whether to buy pants or dresses?" As if unable to make the leap that you, cisgendered female, gender-queer boi, would never wear a dress, teehee. And this may mean you have a different framework entirely for what sex and gender mean, and what freedom you want for your baby.

In our conversations, our child is a she, and sometimes a he. They are an unsexed pea shoot, all juicy green stalk and delicate leaves and clasping whorls of miniature branches. We talk about how we must weed for our own homophobias, face front-on what would make us subtly bend spirals. How our community seems to be more comfortable with the idea of dyke girls than fairy boys. How, boy or girl, masculinity seems more neutral and more celebrated, whereas femininity is suspect still. Would it make people—would it make me—mildly uncomfortable for us to put our infant son in a dress (like my mother did with my brother—much easier for diaper changes anyway)? And our girl—we will dress her in swim trunks for the pool and never pierce her ears unless she asks us too, but can we also put her in flouncy dresses? Do we have to carefully toe the line of not too much gender to make sure the options are open? Or can we seed it all—a riot of hot red zinnias and purple thistle and yellow roses, blue bushels of hydrangeas, creamy callas.

I don't need wooing anymore; loving this is easy, counting down to holding a baby against me. But it's a loving that is like a little blue boat sitting on the green algae of a swampy pond. A little blue boat gliding lightly over fear—fear that is patient and passive and hard to see the bottom of. Is this what parenting is? In these first few years of loving you, I haven't stopped looking over the edge but have felt safe in the contours of the life we've created. Being pregnant, I am rocking and swaying and humbled by the thought of making another person whose existence will matter so much to me.

And we will at first be the only thing that matters to this baby, our voices and smells and the racket of our lives that is the only thing it has ever known or that has ever mattered. It is our big bang and we are the earth it created for itself.

That, I'm not afraid of though. I feel only a great gentleness toward our future selves, selves I know we both have within us. I watch you these days not only as a lover; I watch you and imagine the parent of our child.

You hunched over your guitar; your tenderness when you turn to me, open-faced; the competence of your focused hands. I look at you and I feel ready.

———

Moki Macías was born in Taos, New Mexico. Moki grew up between the high desert of Northern New Mexico and rainy Oregon, and has called Atlanta, Georgia, home since 2006. She is a five-foot-tall femme queer powerhouse whose vocation is community-driven urban planning and advocacy for equitable development. She attended Mount Holyoke College in South Hadley, Massachusetts, and received a master's degree in city and regional planning from Georgia Institute of Technology. She lives with her honey, big dog, and four kitties in a little old house and spends most of her time going to community meetings, taking walks, and making dinner with their big happy chosen family. They are expecting a new addition to the tribe in September 2014.

Story Reflection Questions

1. What is one moment in the story that stayed with you?

    _____

    _____

    _____

2. What questions did you find yourself asking as you read the story?

    _____

    _____

    _____

3. What challenged you about the story?

    _____

    _____

    _____

4. What surprised you about the story?

    _____

    _____

    _____

5. How does this story relate to your own life experience?

    _____

    _____

    _____

My Story from Both Sides of the Exam Table

Debbie Bamberger

When I was nineteen and a sophomore in college in Worcester, Massachusetts, I responded to an ad in the local paper for phone volunteers at Planned Parenthood. I already had an affinity for Planned Parenthood. My mother's life story included a visit to the Margaret Sanger Clinic in Manhattan at nineteen to get a diaphragm, and I had gone to Planned Parenthood to get a diaphragm myself in my hometown of Poughkeepsie when I was still in high school. Volunteering at my local clinic was a life-changing experience for me. I met women working there who opened my eyes to sexism and misogyny. I loved speaking on the phone to women seeking an abortion, providing help to them, and I appreciated the easy availability of birth control and emergency contraception.

I knew how to prevent pregnancy and wanted to, but I was also more careless in college than I had been in high school. I haven't thought too much about my reasons for this, but I may have been testing myself and my fertility, or I may have felt cocky about the ability to have an abortion if I needed one. I had a lot of sex and took emergency contraception many times, back at a time when that meant a huge dose of regular birth control pills and subsequent nausea. But I lucked out and didn't get pregnant.

After college, I moved to San Francisco, thinking it would just be for a year. I had continued working at Planned Parenthood for the rest of college, so it was easy, a week after moving to California, to get a job as a medical assistant and counselor with an ob-gyn who provided abortions. I loved it. I learned so much about abortion, about women's reasons for having abortions, about being nonjudgmental, and about life. Around that time, I was off hormonal birth control and wanting to use more "natural" methods. I got a cervical cap and took the natural family planning class offered at the clinic I worked in. I was twenty-two, living in San Francisco, supporting myself, enjoying my work, making friends, and loving life.

I met a guy named Marcus, a photographer working in a commercial photography studio with my roommate. We were young and hot for each other. I was using the cervical cap for birth control at times when my fertility-awareness methods told me I was fertile and occasionally taking emergency contraception if I messed up.

One day, when my period was late, I took a pregnancy test at work. I'll never forget the feeling of dread when I saw that second line. I remember taking the thirty-three Stanyan bus home and calling Marcus. One of the things about that week that stays with me to this day is that it didn't feel like I had a choice to make. I was pregnant and I wanted it out of me as soon as possible.

The doctor I had worked with for almost a year was skilled, kind, and nonjudgmental, and though I was sheepish and embarrassed, I asked him if he would give me an abortion. I didn't want anyone at work to know, so Marcus met me there at five o'clock in the evening and we went into one of the exam rooms after the rest of the staff had gone home. By that point I'd been in the procedure room for probably a couple hundred abortions, so I knew exactly what to expect, but I didn't know how much it would hurt. I have one of those cervixes where even taking a Pap smear sample feels like my guts are being scraped. The dilation and the suction were really, really painful, and I was barely five weeks. But it was over quickly and I went home feeling relieved.

I entered the first-ever class of the University of California San Francisco Master's Entry Program in Nursing and graduated in 1994 as a women's health nurse practitioner. I moved to Merced, California, to participate in the National Health Service's loan repayment program for physicians and nurses to work in underserved areas while getting their student loans paid off for free.

The dating options for a young, Jewish, professional woman in the Central Valley were few. I met a guy one day while pumping gas at adjoining pumps, and we went out. He lived in Stockton and was an attorney. He came to my place after a date and we had sex on my living-room floor. I knew we needed to use a condom, but we started without one. About ten days later, one day late for my period, I took a test at my clinic. The positive line wrecked me. I hadn't been worried about that one time we had sex, because I didn't think he had come inside me. I called him from my office, ashamed at myself and pissed off at him. Once again, I didn't feel like I had a choice to make; I just wanted the pregnancy over as soon as possible. I was living in Merced, and no one did abortions there. I had two ob-gyn colleagues I respected, and even though I knew they didn't do abortions, I knew they were *capable* of doing aspirations, but neither of them would. I was ashamed to admit to them that I was pregnant, being a responsible women's health provider, but I felt trapped in my small town and needed to ask them. One of them was very skittish about abortion and didn't really believe in it, though he seemed supportive of my decision. The other just didn't know how he would do it logistically. We didn't have the equipment in the clinic, and it wasn't possible to do it at the local hospital. When they said no, I had to figure something else out.

I called the doctor I used to work for in San Francisco and made an appointment, but his receptionist called me to cancel because the doctor was stuck in a surgery. Having worked in abortion already for quite a few years, I didn't want to go to the clinic in a nearby city because I'd heard that the skill level of the providers was unpredictable.

My friend from nurse practitioner school was working at San Francisco General and she asked her boss, the medical director, if he would take care of me as a favor to her. He agreed to see me at the end of his day. He was the chief of obstetrics and gynecology at that time and a superstar in the field of family planning and abortion. I'd heard about him but had never met him. He came across as exceptionally kind and accepting. My friend went in with me. The Stockton dude offered to come, but I didn't want him there and never saw him again. My ex-boyfriend Steve came with me though. The procedure went fine—I chose to get some narcotics this time—and I tried not to feel too ashamed, but I really did. I felt one

141

abortion was "acceptable," but two, especially for someone working in the field, was absolutely not. I never talked about it or told anyone.

After my loan repayment commitment was finished, I moved back to the Bay Area as soon as I could. I got a job working for the doctor I'd worked for before graduate school, who had done my first abortion, and shortly thereafter I was hired to work at San Francisco General as a nurse practitioner in contraceptive clinical trials. My boss was the same doctor who had performed my abortion at San Francisco General. It had been a year or two since he'd seen me as a patient, and he didn't acknowledge having ever seen me before when we met for my interview. I thought about saying something to him, thanking him for the positive medical experience I had had with him, but I decided to let it go and hope that he knew from our excellent working relationship that I appreciated him. I spent the next seven years working there, running the birth-control trials, working in the teen family planning clinic, and doing preoperative exams in the abortion clinic for women having second-trimester abortions.

I was very committed to abortion access, and I had been ruminating for several years on the idea of nurse practitioners being able to perform abortions. This is something my friends and nursing professors had talked about in graduate school, but the law in California prohibited it. I was a skilled clinician at this point, very good at laminaria placement (laminaria are dilator sticks that are placed into the cervix the day before an abortion to dilate the cervix gently) and teaching ob-gyn residents how to do contraceptive implant insertions and removals. I asked my boss if he would consider training me to do surgical abortions. He told me that if I was moving to Montana or someplace like that he would consider it, but since we lived in the Bay Area there really wasn't a need. It was also against the law for anyone other than a physician to perform an abortion in California at that time, and I believed that this doctor, while fervently pro-choice, was a very moral person and would never consciously break a law. I felt mixed, but not surprised, about his response. He was always very overt about respecting my clinical skills and judgment, but the fact that he wasn't interested in helping me push my profession ahead was sad but not unpredictable.

I continued to work at San Francisco General, and during that time I got married. After I had my first baby in 2002 and we moved to Berkeley, I decided to stop commuting to the city, and I was hired by

Planned Parenthood in Richmond. It felt so good to be back at a Planned Parenthood, where the seeds had been planted at age nineteen for my interest in reproductive health. I told my immediate supervisor that I had a long-term goal of helping nurse practitioners be able to do abortions. I didn't think too much about it after that, but one day the medical director of our affiliate called me and said, "I heard you want to do abortions. When do you want to come train with me?" Planned Parenthood as an organization was thinking about access and what to do if Roe v. Wade was overturned and had begun planning for "miscarriage management": training advanced practice clinicians to do uterine aspirations for miscarriages or failed medication abortions to ensure that we had the skills that might someday be needed.

I began my training in 2005. I took to it right away. I have good hands and lots of experience inside the uterus, and I was passionate about it. I was floored by the power I felt I had to change a woman's life in the process of a five- to ten-minute procedure. We had to be creative about working within the limitations of the law—I learned to do all parts of the procedure, but the doctor would begin the suction part of the process and then I could take over to complete it.

I found out that two researchers at UCSF were starting a study to look at training advanced practice clinicians to be abortion providers. I had already done about a hundred procedures by then. One of the researchers at UCSF had been my professor and knew that I had been trained, so she asked me if I'd be willing to be the study's first official trainee. I was overjoyed. Their goal was to use the data to help change California's physician-only law. It took about seven years, but it worked. The researchers collected data on about 13,000 procedures, proving that advanced practice clinicians could perform first-trimester abortions as safely and with as much patient satisfaction as our physician counterparts. As of January 1, 2014, after having completed five hundred procedures over the course of the study, I'm a legal first-trimester aspiration abortion provider. I feel so proud of participating in the study and the process of changing the law.

Meanwhile, in my nonwork life, I've been in a book group with six other women for the past eight years. We know each other pretty well. Last year, my book group participated in a research study looking at women's conversations about abortion. We read a book of essays and then had a discussion about the book, which turned into a conversation about personal pregnancy experiences, including abortion. All the women in my book group knew I was an abortion provider beforehand, but only one knew that I had had an abortion. The conversation made me realize that, although I am working to help normalize and destigmatize abortion, I'm not at all "out" about my own abortions. I didn't reveal that I had had an abortion until pretty far into the discussion, after another, older member of the book group disclosed her abortion. The book group conversation made me think about the stigma around abortion. In my experience, it doesn't have to be, and shouldn't be, a gut-wrenching, heartbreaking decision-making process. I asked myself and my book group friends, "If abortion is part of one out of three women's lifetime experiences, why not treat it like getting your period for the first time, getting dumped, or getting in a minor fender-bender? It's something that happens to many of us, we remember it, it impacts our lives, maybe even changes our lives, but it doesn't ruin our lives or make us have to hang our heads in shame." The women in my book group agreed. Stigma hurts us.

When I thought about writing this story, I was nervous. Nervous about using my real name, about others being able to identify some of the people in my story, identifying myself as an abortion provider, and acknowledging my abortions. I didn't want people who think highly of me to know that I had had abortions. But after thinking about it a lot, I decided that being open about my experiences felt better than hiding. I hope other women, both the women in my life and the women I take care of, will have the freedom to speak out too.

Debbie Bamberger is a women's health nurse practitioner at Planned Parenthood in the Bay Area. Originally from Hopewell Junction, New York, she has lived in California for twenty-five years. She is a cofounder of the Women's Community Clinic in San Francisco. Debbie has accomplished much in her twenty-year career, but her proudest accomplishments are her two sons. She lives with them and her husband in Berkeley, California.

Story Reflection Questions

1. What is one moment in the story that stayed with you?

   _____

   _____

   _____

2. What questions did you find yourself asking as you read the story?

   _____

   _____

   _____

3. What challenged you about the story?

   _____

   _____

   _____

4. What surprised you about the story?

   _____

   _____

   _____

5. How does this story relate to your own life experience?

   _____

   _____

   _____

A Body Worthy of Desire

Sean Saifa M. Wall

Since the day I was born, my body has defined my experience, commitment, and activism. At the age of twenty-five, I received my medical records from Columbia-Presbyterian Medical Center. After months of waiting, unreturned phone calls, and lost medical record request forms, I finally got a manila envelope in the mail, opened it, and began scanning the dense packet of information. I read doctors' notes, surgeons' notes, and other information related to my birth. The records included the length of my phallus along with descriptions of my scrotum and palpable, but undescended, testicles. The doctors also noted that I had "ambiguous" genitalia, which was later crossed out and replaced with "normal." Based on the size of my genitals and the medical community's commitment to the gender binary, I was assigned female. In the records was written:

> In the interest of proper psychosexual orientation of the infant, and in order to protect the parents' emotional well-being, the mother has been told that:

1. The baby is a girl and will function as such.
2. She has gonads that require removal in the future (not testes).

My mother would later tell me that when she brought me home from the hospital, the Pediatric Endocrinology Clinic at Columbia-Presbyterian

---

harassed her for a couple of weeks about bringing me in for surgery to remove my undescended testes. She wondered, *Why are these people harassing me so much?* My mother's resistance alone spared me from surgery until I was much older.

I was a rambunctious and curious kid. I ran around the house shirtless, beating my chest with declarations that I was a boy. I thought I was a boy until I was seven and my mom, through words and dresses, reinforced my assignment as female. I hated dresses with a passion and would always reach for my corduroy overalls in place of a dress any day.

I always marveled at the size of what doctors referred to as an "enlarged clitoris," and I knew the bodies of my female playmates were different from mine. Whenever they saw my "clitoris" they remarked at its appearance and were amazed that I could pee standing up. This bathroom ability distinguished me from other girls and, despite my mother's efforts, confirmed for me that I was indeed a boy.

When I was eight years old my mom talked to me about having "testicular feminization syndrome." Of course, at that age I didn't know what that was or what that meant for my body. I didn't know how different I was until my period failed to arrive. One morning at the age of eleven, I had spots of blood in my underwear and I thought that my period had finally come. I was living with my sister in North Carolina at the time, and she told me that young women get their period around my age. I was scared. I didn't know what to do. She bought me maxi pads and advised me to wear them during my period. I only used one. The trickle of blood stopped, and since I didn't have any more signs of menstruation, there was nothing more to talk about. I don't have a medical explanation for it, but from what I understand it's just something that weirdly happens.

My intersex trait would resurface again when a painful urinary tract infection landed me in a doctor's office. The doctor told my sister that she "did not observe a vagina." My sister told the doctor about the trait in my family now known as androgen insensitivity syndrome (AIS).

I am one of seven people in my family living with this trait. AIS is an intersex trait where the infant is born with XY chromosomes and undescended testicles, but the external genitalia appear female, ambiguous, or as an underdeveloped male. There are variations in the severity of AIS that range from complete androgen insensitivity syndrome (CAIS) to mild androgen insensitivity syndrome (MAIS). I fell somewhere in the middle, having been exposed to androgens in the womb. However, in the eyes of my doctors, I did not masculinize "enough" to be assigned male.

So much of me was shrouded in secrecy. Because of pain related to my undescended testicles, they were removed when I was thirteen. Barely out of surgery, and in excruciating pain, a team of residents came into my room to look at the fresh wounds and, also, to examine my genitals.

I was not only subject to an invasive medical procedure, I was doubly violated by the prying eyes of mostly male residents examining my half-naked pubescent body.

These examinations, borne of curiosity and fascination, continued for me as an adult when physicians would often want to get a look at my genitals even when my visit was for something totally unrelated, like asthma.

I didn't find out the specifics of my birth until sophomore year of college when I searched "testicular feminization syndrome" online. The information that came up on the screen referred to testicular feminization syndrome as androgen insensitivity syndrome. Reading the descriptions of the physical characteristics of people with AIS, I was both shocked and relieved: a combination that left me profoundly sad and afraid. That was perhaps my worst semester in college.

I felt paralyzed with this new information, and I avoided sex and dating altogether. Despite being one of the "big dykes on campus," I avoided any sexual contact that involved nudity. Whenever I *did* have sex with women, I touched them. I did not allow them to touch me. That worked for the most part until I was a senior and started dating a woman who was as interested in making love to me as I was to her. Just the thought of that terrified me. Before we had sex for the first time, I tearfully called home, only to meet with my mother's own limitations in explaining how I could negotiate sex with an intersex body. She had no answers for me.

When my new girlfriend and I eventually had sex, we discovered neither of us really knew what we were doing. With the very real disconnection I felt from my own body, and my overall sexual inexperience, I was a horrible lover. After that relationship ended, I continued to have sexual relationships devoid of connection and sexual pleasure.

My relationship with my body and sexuality was colored by the unmonitored prejudices of doctors and by growing up black, poor, and queer, which all contributed to a deep sense of being unlovable.

I chose women who were curious about my body but daunted at the prospect of trying to please me. I didn't have a vagina, a G-spot, a penis, or a prostate. I felt incapable of sexual pleasure.

I didn't experience my first orgasm until the age of twenty-five. Prior to taking testosterone, I would fantasize about women and sex, but I didn't have any sexual urges since I didn't have any sex hormones in my body. My first orgasm was with a woman who was patient with me and advocated for my pleasure. She listened to my body's rhythm with every move that she made. Before her, I did not feel desired or worthy of the time it might take not only for me to orgasm but for my different body to be explored with respect.

I moved to the Bay Area when I was twenty-four, legally changed my name, started taking testosterone, and reaffirmed my gender as male. The transition to manhood was a leap of faith. I decided to transition because I felt my body already moving in that direction prior to my testicles being removed at thirteen. My transition was an act against the path prescribed for me by the medical community. For the most part, infants with androgen insensitivity syndrome are assigned female, but in reality at least 20 percent of those assigned female will transition to live as male.

The physical part of my transition was not easy. As my trans* brothers were celebrating the gender-affirming effects of testosterone, I was experiencing the estrogenic effects of excess testosterone, such as tender breasts, water retention, and weight gain. My body was reacting that way because of my partial sensitivity to testosterone. I soon realized that *my* transition as an intersex person was different. It was then that I started to identify more with being an intersex person, distinguishing myself from the trans* community. For the longest time, the FTM[5] community provided a space for me to connect with other men who were raised and socialized as female, but I realized that I needed to step out and claim my place as an intersex man in this world.

---

5 FTM stands for female-to-male. FTM describes a transgender or transsexual person who was assigned female at birth and knows that their gender identity is male. This process is often referred to as transitioning from female-to-male (FTM).

When I discovered masturbation, I started to connect with my intersex body and became more determined than ever to reclaim it. The unfamiliar became known, and the estranged part of me came home. I felt more confident. I was emboldened by my newfound sexual freedom. I learned how to touch myself and masturbated all the time. I felt like a young person experiencing puberty. Over time, my focus on masturbation became an obsession, and I unknowingly started to feed my growing addiction to sex.

It started with responding to sexual ads posted on Craigslist. Then I started watching porn. The obsession with sex was not confined to the privacy of my mind or my bedroom, but spilled out into my office and work life. Like the addict that I was, the signs were painfully obvious that my life was spinning out of control. The justification for all of this was that I had been denied this pleasure for so long and, eventually, I would tire out and move on. Over time, though, it became clear that no matter how much sex I had, it was never enough.

By the time I sought professional help, I couldn't think straight. I was walking around in a haze of confusion and sadness. I felt alone. I was having an affair with a coworker, flirting with a married woman, and having sex with people I met online. I eventually "bottomed out" and talked to a woman at my job who was also a therapist. She recommended several therapists. By sheer chance, I randomly chose one who had over fifteen years in sexual recovery. After hearing me talk about my sordid sexual life, he pointed me toward a twelve-step program for sexual addiction. At first, I refused to believe I was an addict of any kind. After only a handful of meetings, I began to see that my life had become unmanageable as a result of my sexual pursuits. I eventually shed many of those behaviors with the help of a sponsor, meetings, and working the steps, leaving me with the challenge of building a healthy sexuality that did not rely on external validation.

I know my sexual addiction is not a *result* of being born with AIS. I suspect, though, it might be a *byproduct* of the prejudicial medical treatment I received and unaddressed trauma. My addiction to sex is a function of the violence that I witnessed both at home and in my community. This manifested as cycles of substance use, incarceration, and dysfunctional interpersonal relationships. However, one of the more resounding messages that I received from society and medical providers was that my black, queer, working-class, intersex body was not enough. From an early age I was told that my body was different. Doctors told my mother that my intersex status was not to be discussed with anyone except other doctors. Many times in a doctor's office I would lie there as they examined my genitals in ways that were unapologetic and disrespectful. Unfortunately, these are not isolated experiences. So many of my friends with intersex traits have been subjected to the same treatment or have endured much worse.

Although our bodies may have been altered from their unique and faultless beginnings, we are worthy of being held, pleasured, and explored with respect and boundaries. In short, fulfilled.

I say to myself and other intersex people reading this: We are worthy of deep desire and profound respect. The journey home has not been easy.

In a radical awakening of our sexual desires and prowess, we have the right to choose celibacy or not, kink or vanilla, top/bottom or switch, monogamy or polyamory, queerness or nonqueerness. I demand our right to be fully incorporated and embodied human beings.

———

Sean Saifa M. Wall is an intersex activist, writer, collage artist, and somatic practitioner in training. He hails from the Bronx and spent nine years in the Bay Area, California, before moving to Atlanta, Georgia. He is currently the board president of Advocates for Informed Choice, a legal rights organization dedicated to protecting the bodily integrity of intersex infants. You can find him on Twitter or Facebook as well as on Tumblr at saifaemerges.tumblr.com. When he is not on the road traveling for work or pleasure, you can find him in Atlanta's Westview community.

Story Reflection Questions

1. What is one moment in the story that stayed with you?

    _____

    _____

    _____

2. What questions did you find yourself asking as you read the story?

    _____

    _____

    _____

3. What challenged you about the story?

    _____

    _____

    _____

4. What surprised you about the story?

    _____

    _____

    _____

5. How does this story relate to your own life experience?

    _____

    _____

    _____

So Small

Yania Escobar

I woke up in the living room, my palms against the soft couch fabric. My housemate Patrick was looking at me, his head slightly retracted and eyes wide open like two big blue nazars, the kind that keep the evil eye away. Little by little, the memories of the previous hour came back. I was on the bed, feeling the memory foam contour to my body, a tremendous pressure on my hips and a closing at my throat. I had seen him, his greasy hair strands hanging over his reddened face and arms stretched with hands clasping my neck. I looked at the silly mushroom tattoo on his arm above my face. Just before that, a friend had come to show us his amazing bag of weed. "That's not even funny," I said right before he dragged me to the room to choke me.

I don't know why I stayed with my boyfriend. My period was like clockwork, so I knew something was up when I missed it. I worked at the free clinic, so I decided to just take a test in the bathroom. I took the warm cup in my hand, walked into an exam room, turned my head to look both ways, and reached for the cold, slick handle to close the door. My friend Rebecca noticed me sneaking around and asked, "What are you up to?"

"I'll tell you later," I said and heard the smooth click of the door. I was certain of a lot. I knew I was pregnant. I knew my IUD had failed. I knew it was so small, and it was inside.

I felt a strange sense of warmth on my chest and a heaviness at my feet. No knots in my stomach or stirring in my gut. I told Rebecca and said I did not know what I would do. Now that I look back, I can almost see our bodies standing in that messy clinic room. I can see the top of my head and I feel a combination of excitement, pity, and disbelief. I am not inside. My friends assured me that an abortion would be justified in this case, since my birth control had failed, but I was conflicted.

A few days later I was in Drew's apartment upstairs. His beard prickled my cheek as I lay on my back on the rough plastic kitchen table. His heavy hand covered my mouth, hushing our voices as they disappeared into the complete darkness of the room. He liked to ponder the dishonor of our affair seconds after we finished having sex. I was not sure whose genes had combined with mine inside my womb.

"Baby! Where are you?"

"Shit. Be right back," I said to Drew and went downstairs.

Dan, my boyfriend, was in the backyard looking for me. He heard my steps on the wooden stairs and came to meet me. His lips touched mine and his breath tasted of Four Loko and spliffs. His left eyelid hung lower than his right, and his lips drooped at the corners. We made our way inside the room, and he lay down on our bed. I saw his body jerk and heard the guttural hack. I made it back just in time with a bowl to hold his rejected alcohol and saw his blood on the mattress. His nose was bleeding. I got him some tissue and sat next to him with one hand on the mattress and the other's fingers sliding through thin strands of hair. My hand on the mattress felt a flow of tepid fluid, and the scent of ammonia filled my nose. He peed the bed twice the week he found out I was pregnant.

The night I told him, he blurted out, "Well, you're gonna have an abortion, right?" I went to bed alone, hearing the faint sounds of explosions and shooting that came from the game console all night. It was not that different from any other night, or the nights I moved my hands stealthily under the sheets, illuminated by the light of my phone. "Don't get me wrong, I would fuck the shit out of you," Drew had texted.

"Roughly or gently?"

"Both, now stop, you're gonna get me in trouble."

The second time Dan peed the bed I sat on the coarse carpet, my knees bent under the weight of my thighs, his voice thundering above me. "My mom would've found clean sheets!"

I asked Drew if he heard his yells, and he came downstairs. Drew bent my legs so that my thighs rested on my belly. His palm gently found my mouth; I relaxed and took him in whole. He did not want me to have the baby in fear that it was his. I was not sure; it was still so small.

I called my friend Jackie because I knew she chose to have a child when everyone around her told her not to. I met her at the back room in the clinic; the bittersweet taste of chocolate filled my mouth. "Once I saw the plus sign, I knew I was going to be a mother," she said quickly with a smile on her face.

That day, I sent out a blood pregnancy test, I wanted to know what "the count" would be, knowing deep inside I was trying to justify my inevitable decision. I was already taking prenatal vitamins and told my college counselor that I would become a parent. I watched her pull out a sheet from a file cabinet and heard the sound of her pen sliding across the paper. It was winter break, she said, no matter what I chose to do I would need referrals.

When Dan and I got to the ultrasound clinic, the pressure in my bladder caused my eyes to tear up. A woman of gentle gestures brought us into a room and asked me to lie down on the cushioned table beside the white screen. I felt a cold, long instrument against my cervix. On the screen I saw a thin, rough ring of whiteness and a tiny spec at the top. The woman could not find a heartbeat. So small.

After that appointment, I had a long phone conversation with Drew while sitting on the fire hydrant next to the post office; I could see my reflection on the glass windows. I was there to mail my mother a Christmas present, no news attached. I made an abortion appointment for December 29, before it grew any bigger.

I was pro-choice, until the choice was mine. Abortion was a wonderful technological advance that "just wasn't for me," but some of my best friends had had them, I was sure!

The night I told Dan, he called me a baby killer. I felt as if all our days together had amounted to this. That time he had thrown my car key on the roof of an apartment building. My feet slipped on the granulated shingles as my outstretched arms cut the wind to find some balance. The time I felt the spice of Tapatio flowing down my face as he emptied the bottle on me. How I felt when he followed me into the shower and stroked me on the left temple. I saw the small rectangular bathroom window all around me, a sense of déjà vu and birth and death, and then just dreams.

All my dreams at a standstill. I had withdrawn the semester at school so we could find a place to sleep other than the hard concrete of the sidewalk next to the church. I dreamed of waking up to something other than a cop's shiny black boot pressed against my body telling me I couldn't sleep there. My immigration status prohibited the state from providing me with financial aid for college. When I flunked out, going back to my parents' house was not a choice. They had not brought me to this country of opportunity just before high school to watch me fail and walk all night talking to myself, inhaling the smokes and fumes of the city. All dreams.

The morning of my abortion appointment, I woke up in our new apartment to the sound of shiny boots on concrete coming from the TV. I could swear I dreamed of the enemy from the game he was playing all night. I walked to the bathroom and turned on the shower. I let in the piercing sound of water drops smacking the ceramic floor and soon felt them embrace me as I looked at the little rectangular window. I came out wrapped in a towel to find him gone. Patrick, my roommate, said he had gone to exchange a bong downtown. He would have taken my car if the police had not gotten to it first. I did not have permission to drive on this planet because I was an alien.

At the clinic, a woman in scrubs watched my salty tears find my clenched lips. "It seems like you need more time…" she said after printing out the pictures of the white ring. I had to do it before it got any bigger. Drew was texting me as I sat in the waiting room, blankly staring at a "celebrities are just like us" page of a magazine. I felt the vibration of his concern in my pocket as I signed some papers. I wished I could feel his rough beard on my cheek then. I took some pills and let them dissolve against my cheeks. The chalky pieces swished in my mouth, and my face was dry.

I looked at my prescription and frowned. "How much is this going to hurt?"

The nurse shook her head swiftly and paused. "Oh, it's going to hurt."

I had given Drew's phone number as my contact because it was the only number I knew by heart, and because I wished he would have the courage to be there.

On my way out, I called Rebecca and told her where I was, what I had done, and what I needed from her. My shoulders dropped when I saw her little blue car approaching. I sat on the stiff seat and she drove me to her house. I stood in the living room, looking at the round patterns of the shiny wooden floor and told her about the Tapatío, the pressure on my throat, and the little rectangular window. She let me know she would not give me a ride home unless I grabbed my stuff and took the second pill at her new house.

I slid the key into the door, holding my breath, and came in slowly to find only Patrick in the house. "I'm leaving," I proclaimed, and I packed my clothes in the same brown leather suitcase that my mother and I had packed our clothes in eight years earlier to find a better life. I stuffed my kitty into her pungent black bag and took her scratching post with me.

We parked next to an Ethiopian food restaurant, and I faced my phone screen. I pressed the down arrow until I found him. "I'm leaving. I'm *leaving* leaving." Dan, said he knew I was going to do this to him and a whole bunch of other words that got blended into the flight of the birds above. I saw the blue sky and turned to see Rebecca's freckled face, the corners of her mouth turned upward. I was free.

What followed feels like one of those summer afternoons during carnival when I just wished I had the energy to fill up a water bottle and poke holes in the cap to attack my friends. I thought I would do it without any more pills than were absolutely needed. About an hour after taking the pill, I started to feel uneasiness at the top of my stomach and a sharp ache in my womb. I reached for the orange container that Rebecca had helped me retrieve from the pharmacy. I needed a government ID and did not have one. Rebecca brought me a shiny metal bowl and I held it tightly, but I felt constrained. Drew called again; I told him I would have to talk to him later. "Are you OK?" I heard as my finger found the red button. I pushed on the mattress to get the weight of my torso over my legs. The pad between my legs was heavy, and I knew I needed openness. Slowly, I walked to the bathroom and pushed the door open. I rested my arms on the toilet seat, opened my mouth, and saw the rejected pill floating amid Ethiopian food. My hand found the cold handle and it was all gone. I braced myself, resting my head on my arm. I found the strength to stand up and sit on the toilet. My left arm stretched out to the side and found the faucet; I heard the symphony of drops. I climbed in the bathtub and squatted for what seemed like two hours, feeling the cool water on my back. A knock at the door brought my head back over my shoulders; Rebecca wanted to check on me. I rubbed my body with the white towel, found a new pad, and got dressed. I was feeling light and hot.

Rebecca held me on the futon, and I tried to take another painkiller. She said my phone had been ringing, and I called Drew back. He said he was worried and asked if he could do anything to help. With an even tone, I said I would be fine, but I needed some time. My friend had to go to a dinner party. I was in a stupor and felt my eyes shut.

I woke up to the crisp sunshine of a winter morning. My kitty was sitting next to the window, her eyes closed, head tilted up, and black fur shining white. I heard sounds in the kitchen and felt tension in my stomach. I sat up and saw the huge red stain on the sheets and my face grew warm. I gathered the sheets and headed for the laundry room. The fresh linen smell filled my nose as I pushed the sheets into the washer. I turned my wrist, pressed a button, and forgot about the incident. The mattress was clean. Rebecca came from outside and asked me how I felt. I searched for the words, but settled for "fine." That day I helped her move, my arms shaking under the weight of her desk. The next week, my arms trembled to hold my body off the wooden floor at my capoeira academy. I cleaned those floors so I could take class for a reduced price, and I began my healing journey.

I had called my friend Stephen to ask him if he needed a roommate. He said his son was moving out soon and he would need help with rent. It worked out perfectly. A couple of nights later I was lying with Drew on the sheets he'd brought me. I woke up feeling his lips on my neck. My new room had so many windows, the blossoming tree outside filled my view. "You like to struggle," he said, showing his perfect white teeth.

I went to Planned Parenthood to check in about a week after my abortion. I was feeling relieved like they said I would. I wanted birth control like they said I would. They said I wanted the Depo-Provera shot. I was not sure. I called my mother to consult with her because I had heard that the shot makes people depressed. Her voice was shaky, and she said she did not know. There was a long silence and then someone needed her at work. I was alone when I hung up the phone, and when the needle went in my arm, providing my body with a heavy dose of progesterone. I cried on the bus alone.

When I told her about my abortion, she said, "If the count was not right, and they couldn't find a heartbeat, then what was the point of continuing the pregnancy?" I felt disempowered in my decision to terminate my pregnancy, and we never talked about the subject again.

———

My abortion hurt me. I am glad I did it, but there is still work to be done. I do not know that healing will ever be achieved or that there are wounds to heal. I was empowered to go back to school and finish my interdisciplinary studies major and education minor. My period never regulated for more than two months after the abortion and the shot. I take my temperature in the morning and predict my ovulation, but the blood comes when it wants. After Drew, I had unprotected sex with a variety of men and was lucky to come out of this phase without another abortion. About seven months ago I decided to become celibate until I figure out what I want. I play, I make art, I write, I cry, I talk, and I share my story. I want people to know the real stories and the complexity of our decisions. I am pro-choice and pro-life, depending on whose and what life and choices are being discussed.

———

Yania Escobar was born in Uruguay and moved to the United States at the age of thirteen with her mother. While in college at the University of California, Berkeley, she began to volunteer at the Berkeley Free Clinic as a medic. There she explored her interest in reproductive health by participating in the women and trans shift at the clinic. She was disappointed by the lack of research dedicated to the female reproductive system and lack of agency clients' experience in the health system but excited about the progress that has been made through community organizing. Yania was trained by the Bay Area Doula Project as an abortion doula and by San Francisco General Hospital as a birth doula. She continues her doula education and networking through workshops such as Backline's Pregnancy Options and collaborations with doula projects around the country. She is a massage therapist working in a complementary clinic for low-income women living with cancer. Yania believes in the healing and transforming power of mindful creative movement, art, and human connection. She nourishes her soul by playing capoeira, making art, and maintaining a regular yoga and meditation practice.

Story Reflection Questions

1. What is one moment in the story that stayed with you?

   _____

   _____

   _____

2. What questions did you find yourself asking as you read the story?

   _____

   _____

   _____

3. What challenged you about the story?

   _____

   _____

   _____

4. What surprised you about the story?

   _____

   _____

   _____

5. How does this story relate to your own life experience?

   _____

   _____

   _____

Life Handed Me Lemons, but I'm Making Lemonade Today

Tonya Rosenberg

Tennessee: Living near all my family and friends, right behind my mom and dad (the coolest people alive); first marriage to husband who has severe bipolar disorder and worked the graveyard shift.

In late December of 1993, I went to the doctor for flu-like symptoms—lots of vomiting, to be precise. I have always been the kind of person that can't throw up no matter how bad I feel, unless I've got a *really* bad flu. Turns out I was pregnant, after only three months of trying. I wasn't even far enough along that a home pregnancy test would have been reliable.

Well, the sickness did not contain itself to morning hours, nor did it end with the first trimester. I had hyperemesis gravidarum—a condition that is basically nonstop nausea and vomiting. It can be a very serious condition. During the first trimester alone, I lost forty pounds and was admitted to the hospital for dehydration/malnutrition on five separate occasions…with lots of trips to the ER and even a period when we tried having a nurse come to my home and give me IVs. I remember at one point being so miserable that I begged my doctor to just let me and the baby die. That evening in the hospital I had some sort of blood clot when I went to the bathroom, making me call the doctor immediately to say, "Don't let my baby die." I couldn't keep down so much as a sip of water until we hit upon *three* prescription medications that worked to let me keep liquid—and even some food—down. I had to stay on the medications the entire pregnancy, as I went right back into super-sick mode if I tried to wean off them. I don't remember now all the med names, but I do remember Phenergan having about the same effectiveness as a Tic-Tac.

Other health issues in my pregnancy included gestational diabetes and a bit of high blood pressure in the last couple of weeks. Environmental factors included a large amount of debt and a very unsupportive husband with bipolar disorder who broke his leg in my last trimester, which cut our weekly income in half.

The birth was largely uneventful. When they weighed me in prior to delivery, I weighed less than when I'd conceived. I was induced (I just really wanted to get this pregnancy over with), and from induction to delivery was only about ten hours. I had an epidural (*hooray!*) and an uncomplicated vaginal delivery. After my daughter was weighed and measured, she was taken to the nursery and the health-care team and my husband followed her. I was left alone, and I felt acutely "empty." At the time I thought it was because of being physically empty, of not having my baby in my womb any longer. Looking back, I can see it went far deeper than that.

I struggled with breastfeeding, but baby and mom got into the groove pretty quickly. When Emily was about a week old, I felt she was "breathing funny" and took her to my local ER. The doctors and nurses seemed to be laughing at me, saying that all babies breathe funny. Then the doctor examined Emily and said he'd like to draw some blood. She was only a week old, and I was made to hold down my baby and help someone hurt her. The test results showed that she was very jaundiced. I was told that she'd have to be admitted into the hospital for a couple of days and stay under a bili light. I was also told that lots of babies who are breastfed develop jaundice (which my vulnerable new-mom brain took as, "It's all your fault she's sick"), and she'd be put on a bottle while there. I made them secure a regular room for my daughter, as I was not about to leave her side. The whole time she was there, I never left her. Even to do something as simple as use the bathroom, I'd call a nurse and make her watch Emily until I was finished. I couldn't feed her a bottle, so the nurses had to do it while I sat in the bathroom and tried to keep my sobbing as silent as possible. Part of my inability to handle giving her a bottle was my overwhelming guilt and anxiety, and part was probably that I smelled like the milk she'd had all that time. (At birth, I didn't even let them give her a pacifier or "sugar water"—it was me only.)

Back home, things deteriorated further. I was exhausted but couldn't sleep. I was hyper-alert to her at all times. She slept in the bed with me for nursing purposes (and also because I couldn't put her down for any period of time without panicking), so I never, ever slept deeply. I went days without bathing. I had no appetite, but breastfeeding was something I was determined to do and I had to eat to produce milk. I was afraid to leave the house, and I kept the doors and blinds closed at all times—what I was afraid of I'm not exactly sure. I was manic in my efforts to keep the house and its contents completely clean and could only sit still when nursing. Even then, after she was good at latching on, I would hold her in one arm to nurse while doing chores with the other. My family said I never let her go, but for some reason it was very important to hold her all the time. In hindsight, I now understand that she inherited her father's bipolar disorder, which can cause problems with things like learning to self-sooth.

After some time, I guess I snapped. I'd been having ideas of getting in the car with her, unbelted, and driving into a pole or off a cliff, but the shame and fear of hurting her prevented that. I'd thought about just killing myself, but I couldn't stand the thought of her wondering why I'd done it for the rest of her life, and I couldn't imagine her being raised by her father, who I'd grown to despise during the pregnancy and after the delivery.

One day, Emily was crying (a colicky baby times twenty), and nothing I did soothed her. I was so tired, and so frustrated, and so angry (anger was a *big* part of my life then), that as I was rocking her with my eyes closed, I had what I have to describe as a vision; it was like watching a movie. Her bedroom had white walls, and I saw myself taking this little angel by the ankles and smashing her against the wall until it ran red. My eyes snapped open and I practically ran into her bedroom, put her in the crib as gently as possible, quietly closed her door, walked out of the house, sat in my car, and screamed until I thought my throat was bleeding. When I was all out of tears, I went back inside (she'd fallen asleep) and called my ob-gyn. I have always been "pleasant" and have a hard time asking for help; I don't like to be a bother. That day, though, I was as open and honest about what was happening as I'd ever been about anything. My ob-gyn instructed me to get my mom, who lived very close, to come over and stay with me. The doctor personally called me back later and asked if I could wait until the next day to see her or if I felt I couldn't hold on. My mom had talked me down enough that I felt I could make it another day. (My mom is the best mother I could've ever hoped for, and I am grateful for her presence in my life.) The next day, she accompanied me and the baby to my doctor's office. I was put on Prozac and allowed to continue breastfeeding. I lucked out, and Prozac worked really well for me. I ended up breastfeeding Emily until she was fourteen months old. I really think breastfeeding was my savior, in a strange way. Knowing my little girl refused to take a bottle, knowing that my milk was the only thing that sustained her, made it impossible to do anything that would harm her, including harming myself. I had an incredible support system in my parents, my siblings, and my friends. My then-husband tried his best, but the damage was already done, and we divorced when Emily was three years old.

Washington: No friends or family here except current hubby and daughter; very supportive husband who was financially able to take pretty much the entire pregnancy and the first year of Noah's life off from work.

In March of 1999, I found out I was pregnant. This is also when my husband proposed to me. He hadn't been around for everything the first time around, but I'd informed him as much as I could. I also delved deeply into reading about and researching postpartum mood disorders to prepare myself and him. Again, the primary complaint was being unable to keep anything in my system, but I only had to go to the ER a few times and lost about fourteen pounds in the first trimester. An early ultrasound revealed that I had initially been pregnant with twins but one had failed to thrive and was already being absorbed back into my body. We cried about it, and my husband shared a Jewish tradition in lighting a candle for a soul that couldn't be with us.

We crammed a year's worth of wedding planning into, literally, two months. We also got a new house and had two kitchen renovations during my pregnancy (the old house and the new...*never again!*). In my fifth month, I had major back spasms and had to be carried from the house on a stretcher. It was scary, but they had to give me some major pain and muscle-relaxer meds. There were no available rooms on the mother unit, so I ended up in the cardiac wing, where OB nurses would trek a couple of times a day to monitor mom and baby. At least I know my heart was good and strong!

This time I had gestational diabetes again, but the problems with my blood pressure showed up a lot sooner. I found myself slipping into the old depression/anxiety again toward the end of my pregnancy and was pre-emptively put on Zoloft. During my pregnancy I also worked on a website for women with postpartum mood disorders. (I deal with stress by giving myself more stress, or by throwing myself into helping others, or both.) The delivery was induced again because of the blood-pressure problems. I had the blessed epidural again, and Noah came into the world after only four pushes (guess these big hips *are* good for something!).

The Zoloft did make a positive dent, as did having a lot of knowledge and experience under my belt. I was very lucky to have a supportive husband, but I missed my family very much. I still had the same issues of anxiety and depression and lots of crying, but it was never as severe as my first go-round. I don't remember having any thoughts of harming Noah and only once or twice entertained the idea of harming myself (never as seriously as before—more of an idle thought). The website was doing pretty well, so I also had a lot of other women in similar situations to talk to, which helped a lot.

Today, I'm doing really well. It's 2014, and my daughter is in college. My son will go to high school in the fall. Time has a funny way of marching on like that. I think the postpartum period was just one time of many in my life that showed that I am at risk for mood disorders. Armed with the knowledge I now have, I see how earlier bouts of depression and suicidal thoughts, a serious eating disorder in my youth, childhood sexual abuse, and more contributed to my postpartum depressions. I've also learned that I am a healthier, happier me when I take medication (currently it's Prozac). I continue to work toward removing the stigma of mental health and mood disorders.

I started the Online PPMD Support Group and it's absolutely thriving. We have members from all over the globe. It's sad to think there is such a big need for the website, but it's gratifying to know that so many women and those that care for them are being supported. If I can prevent even one woman from hurting herself or her child, if I can encourage even one woman to go and get treatment, to not be ashamed or afraid…well, that will make all my suffering worth it. I really think in a strange way that having PPMD opened the world up for me. It made me stronger, it made me a fighter, and it gave me a purpose.

———

Tonya Rosenberg grew up on a small dairy farm in Tennessee, where she spent her first 27 years. After going through a difficult pregnancy and postpartum period, and leaving an unhealthy marriage, she moved to the Seattle area. Soon she remarried and became pregnant with her second child in 1999. She searched online for support in her new area, understanding her risk of experiencing postpartum issues again, and found very few mentions of Postpartum Mood Disorders (PPMDs). In an effort to create a support system for herself, and consequently others, she took over a small email group and website which was ready to close. Since its original rebirth in 1999 as The Online PPMD Support Group, this online peer-to-peer support group – the first and largest of its kind – has helped millions of women around the world struggling with PPMDs. Tonya attributes the success of the group to the members themselves, who are incredibly caring and willing to share their struggles and successes. Over the years, the location of the posting forums has changed a few times, but the love and support of moms for each other has remained a beautiful constant. You may visit The Online PPMD Support Group home page at http://www.ppmdsupportpage.com, or go directly to the posting boards at http://postpartumdepression.yuku.com/.

Story Reflection Questions

1. What is one moment in the story that stayed with you?

   _____

   _____

   _____

2. What questions did you find yourself asking as you read the story?

   _____

   _____

   _____

3. What challenged you about the story?

   _____

   _____

   _____

4. What surprised you about the story?

   _____

   _____

   _____

5. How does this story relate to your own life experience?

   _____

   _____

   _____

Becoming a Parent while Trans

Lucía Pérez

In 1994, at the age of thirty, I became a parent for the first time to a baby girl named Viviana. It was also the first time in my life I had been married and living away from home. The marriage lasted for four years after my spouse discovered that I was a homosexual. I moved back home to my mom's house in San Francisco. I kept my job and visited Viviana on a weekly basis while paying for child support. There were visitation and custody battles between Viviana's mom and myself, which hurt the relationship I had with my daughter. In the end, the relationship with both Viviana and her mom ended because of all the drama that occurred every time we came into contact with each other. I haven't seen Viviana in many years, and she doesn't know who I truly am. At least once a week, I take a few minutes to remember her dearly with the hope that someday we will see each other and she will understand and pardon me.

In 1999 I worked for a company that was expanding its services worldwide and developing a new plant in Guadalajara, Mexico. A team of several employees, including myself, took a business trip to Guadalajara to train and assist the new employees. This is when I met the future mother of my two boys, Jonathan and Daniel, who are now thirteen and nine. She was going to work for the Guadalajara plant doing the same work I was doing in the Bay Area. We met during a company meeting in which we were introduced to each other and teamed up together for training. During these training sessions, we ate many lunches and dinners together that soon led to many breakfasts in bed and several trips back to Guadalajara.

In July of 2001, our first boy was born in Guadalajara, but we had to live separate lives until May of 2005 when we were able to live together as a family in San Francisco. Two months later, our second boy was born here in San Francisco. We lived happily married until the day I came out of the closet. For months prior to coming out, I had struggled with my gender identity and sexual orientation in a way I had not struggled before. So much of what I needed was to be fully myself. I could no longer function or focus at home, work, or social settings because my gender identity and sexual orientation made me very self-conscious and very uncomfortable. I came out of the closet at the end of 2009.

Coming out had tremendous consequences, not only for me, but for my family. The home became a graveyard for me; there was a sense of death in the air. Everything I had wished for in my life was gone. I felt the loving relationship and intimacy I had with my spouse dwindle away as the home life we had built together crumbled to the ground. Our living conditions were not the same as before: whereas we used to have fun together, now we hardly spoke. Our hearts were broken, and the children knew it. Feelings of guilt and shame began to build up in me, and I wanted to die.

There were a lot of hurt feelings, especially with my spouse, who could not understand why this was happening to us. During one of our arguments, my spouse yelled at me and called me an old faggot. I thought I would never hear that from her.

Tensions in the home often ran rampant. She was hurt and would take her anger out on the kids and me. Many times I had to intervene between her and the kids because she had lost control. I would get yelled at for intervening and trying to be a parent to my kids. She could not begin to understand why the fuck I did what I did. When I came out to her there was not much said. She wanted answers. She asked me many questions, like how could I be so thoughtless and uncaring of her and the kids? Why had I not told her about this before she got herself into this relationship? What would her mother and father think? What would her friends and neighbors say? What would we do now? Where would we go from here?

These questions passed through my head all day and all night. I tried explaining to her what was happening to me in the best way I knew how, but I didn't have clear answers to many of the questions, and that frustrated me even more. I wanted to go away and die. I cried day and night thinking about what a monster I must be, doing this to my family and doing what I had done to my daughter, Viviana, years earlier. I twice attempted suicide at home and was taken to the psychiatric ward both times.

The words *I'm sorry* had no value or meaning to me at all. I could not think of the words to explain to her and my kids the hell and the pain I felt inside for having caused them pain and inconveniences. I felt I didn't deserve to live and always contemplated ways of killing myself.

Not very long after all these things had happened, I began therapy sessions with a clinical social worker. My depression had worsened by the time I started therapy, and I had been taken off of the two jobs I had at the time.

Before I knew it, I had sunk into and was diagnosed with major depressive disorder and gender identity disorder (now called gender dysphoria). Being home at the time was an unhealthy situation for me and for my family, so I decided I needed to be alone and went away to a shelter for six months. I didn't see much of the kids during this time. I didn't think it was a good idea.

During the two years of therapy and "transitioning" from male to female, I had very little contact with my kids. My medical condition didn't allow me to be in the role of parent, and the kids didn't allow it either. At the time I felt I was just another kid needing even more care and attention than my own kids.

Although I had broken my partner's heart, she didn't pack up and leave. I expected that she would, but instead she hung around and gradually came to the understanding that this wasn't something I wanted to do, but something I needed to do, and that I was born with it and had to live with it for the rest of my life. She understood I needed support. We weren't living together but sometimes we sat down for meals as a family. She made sure I had food to eat, clean clothes and helped me remember to pay my bills and call my mother.

After returning from the shelter, I decided it was time to start living and presenting as a woman 24/7. When my spouse saw what was happening, she gave me a set of rules for dressing up, specifically for when I knew the kids were going to be around. She demanded that I not wear makeup, dresses, skirts, and skimpy clothing anywhere near the kids. Sometime after leaving the shelter I decided it was time to begin hormone replacement therapy and change my legal name to Lucia. So I did.

When the kids saw me wearing a bra and feminine clothing, they took several steps back and quietly disappeared. They complained to their mom about me wearing women's clothing and asked why I was doing it. Their mom prohibited me from explaining to them, saying that I would cause psychological damage to them if I did. She told them that I was a little sick. She told them to respect me, to not say ugly things to me like "you're crazy" and "you're stupid." The kids started to hate me. They were hurt too because they no longer had a dad who played ball, wrestled them down to the ground, and had pillow fights with them. The day came when Jonathan, my older son, also called me a faggot, which made me cry and feel even more depressed. But I understood his pain.

For a long time, I tried to help my sons by looking for therapy for them, without success. I knocked on doors here and there, but for one reason or another we did not qualify for services. It would have been easier if we could have afforded to pay for it. Since I was unemployed for two years due to my medical condition, I took the kids to school every morning and picked them up in the afternoons. This was the only time we spent together, and they didn't like it at all. They didn't talk or listen to me. Many times they told me to go away.

Soon I noticed that they didn't want to be seen with me when I took them to or from school. We would walk to school on most mornings unless it was raining or if we were late. They would not sit with me on the bus. They would not listen to me when I asked them to sit with me. When we got off the bus, they would run to school so their friends wouldn't see them with me. They did the same thing when we walked to school. The last block they would run toward the school. Soon they took it as a fun thing to do and would be laughing and laughing as they did it.

The time came when their friends at school started asking questions about me. Jonathan began to experience incidents of bullying at school. We began to receive complaints about his behavior toward other children and his teachers. He wasn't doing his homework and his grades started slipping. The incidents of bad behavior went on at school and at home until one day he decided to tell us what was happening. He told us he was being bullied at school; the kids were saying that his dad was gay and calling him gay as well.

His mom then prohibited me from coming anywhere near his school or my other boy's school. For me, this was another shot to the heart. My symptoms and issues with guilt, shame, and depression were always being sparked by my kids and their mom. At the time, I was still very sensitive to homophobia and transphobia.

We brought the bullying issues to the attention of the school and social workers, and with their help a safe space was created for Jonathan. Until it all started happening again and we had to move him from that school to one where nobody would know his dad.

Communication between us gradually improved after placing Jonathan in another school and beginning therapy together.

Daniel's reaction to me coming out was nothing like Jonathan's. Daniel never asked me any questions, but he kept himself distant from me and still does to some extent. He has asked his mom many times why I dress the way I do, why we no longer live together, and when we will live together again. He's never said a word to me about my transition.

As time went by and after many months of therapy sessions, my sons and I have developed a better relationship, a relationship that has allowed us to exchange dialogue, have a few laughs, and even play ball together sometimes. But better hasn't been enough. My older son still hasn't gotten over losing the unique relationship we had, and as a result still has behavioral problems that have affected his performance at school. He has told his mom many times that he is hurt by what happened to us as a family, that he misses the old me, and that he wishes we all lived together again as a family. My youngest son, Daniel, also misses his old dad. He's also told his mom many times that he would like us to live together again.

I don't miss being who I was before, but I miss being a parent to my children and what we had together as a family. I miss how little they once were. I miss the times when I got home from work and Daniel would be at the window waiting for me and would run downstairs to greet me. The house was always clean and welcoming, with fresh, hot food on the table. Eating together was a lot of fun. I miss when we played ball together at the park and the times I walked both of them to and from school.

Now they're big kids and have changed in some ways, but I love them just as much. Whenever they get in trouble at school I feel that I'm responsible for it. I also wish the four of us lived together as a family again. Their mother and I have talked about it many times, and we are currently in the process of moving in together. It hasn't been possible because of lack of work and money, but that's the plan.

Now their mother and I talk on the phone every day to keep up with what the kids are doing at school and at home. I visit them all the time, at least once a week. I still play with them and eat with them, but it's not what it used to be. They're big kids now and behave differently, like older kids.

I love my children dearly, and the plan is to live together with them again. We finally found and qualified for family therapy for LGBT families. Thanks to the support from the LGBT community, the possibility of moving in with them to live together as a family again is becoming more real.

The relationship I had with my children and my spouse will never be what it once was, but the love for each other is still there. That I know. I still love my spouse, but not in the way I used to pretend. I feel that I still love her, but as a lesbian kind of love, a woman-to-woman type of relationship. She would never commit to an intimate relationship again, because in her eyes I am still that guy she met and fell in love with and whom she still waits upon to come home again.

Knowing how the kids and my spouse feel about me coming out of the closet and living as a woman has always made me feel guilty and ashamed of who I am, and it still does, because I saw how they suffered. I still sometimes wish I was never born this way or that I had come out of the closet when I was much younger. Yet I feel that although coming out of the closet has been a bittersweet melody, I don't regret it because doing it freed me from living a lie. I hope that in the near future my spouse and I will live together to continue raising our kids, but this time, as two moms.

———

Lucía Pérez was born in Nicaragua into a Catholic family and then migrated to San Francisco 38 years ago. She loves women, nature, animals, fine art, rock music, gothic literature, horror films, and vegan food. Her all-time favorite movie is The Exorcist.

Story Reflection Questions

1. What is one moment in the story that stayed with you?

    _____

    _____

    _____

2. What questions did you find yourself asking as you read the story?

    _____

    _____

    _____

3. What challenged you about the story?

    _____

    _____

    _____

4. What surprised you about the story?

    _____

    _____

    _____

5. How does this story relate to your own life experience?

    _____

    _____

    _____

The Stories We Tell

Katherine Towler

When I turned thirty in 1986, my sister gave me a T-shirt that featured a cartoon woman, one hand held dramatically to her cheek, mouthing the words, "I can't believe it. I forgot to have children." At work the following week, I attended a meeting with my coworkers, all women. Making small talk before we got down to business, one of them asked me what I had received for my birthday. I can still remember the looks on their faces when I described the T-shirt, my favorite gift. There was a moment of stunned and disapproving silence. Finally one of them said, "That's horrible."

At the time, I lived in Manhattan and was single. It wasn't just that I had forgotten to have children. I had forgotten to get married too. My coworkers were sophisticated, urban career women, not the sort who would be expected to react as they did. But I—and the T-shirt—had crossed a line, mocking the sacrosanct notion of children as the ultimate fulfillment.

I did not set out to be a rebel. I am essentially a shy, private person, given to introspection. In most situations, I do my best not to get noticed. Somewhere along the way, however, it became clear that I was not like most other people. I did not want to have children. Though I saw nothing rebellious in this fact of my nature, others seemed to find it if not rebellious then at least subversive, or odd, or sad, or just plain inexplicable.

A friend recently told me the recurring fantasy of her adolescent years. She used to dream about being the mother of five boys. An only child, she wanted to have children and lots of them. She did not imagine her future husband. He would come along at the appropriate time and did not matter too much one way or the other, but she could see those five boys. "A basketball team," she said. "That's what I wanted."

When she asked me if I ever had such fantasies, I was stumped. I played with dolls when I was young and liked dressing up, pretending to be a grown-up woman, but I cannot recall ever imagining the children I would one day have. It wasn't a part of my landscape, a part of the story I told myself.

At the age of eight, I used to sit on the living room couch with a copy of *Reader's Digest*. I would stop when I came to the brightly colored pages of ads and make up stories about the people in the pictures, giving them names and relationships and concocting elaborate scenarios. They might be from Ohio, where my grandmother lived, and have a farm with lots of animals, and maybe there had been an accident with a piece of equipment and someone got hurt. Now they were all running in from the field to get help. They were a ways out of town, and there wasn't time to wait for the ambulance, so the father took the injured child and set him in the backseat of the station wagon. It would turn out only to be a broken leg, nothing major (my stories usually ended happily), but there were some tense moments getting to the hospital.

I have a vivid memory of myself at this age, turning the pages of the magazine, mumbling the words out loud. It wasn't enough to think the stories. I needed to say them to make them real. Like the books I read, my inventions were as real to me, if not more so, than the daily events of my life. The actual world, where I was forced to confront such agonies as gym class and other children my age, was a place full of frightening experiences completely beyond my control. The stories I created were mine, as were the books I read. Here I was master of everything, free to make it come out the way I wanted, free to become someone else through the pages of a book.

I became a writer on those afternoons when I sat on the couch with *Reader's Digest* and gave the two-dimensional people in the ads roles to play and plots to enact. Or maybe I was already a writer, and it was then that I fully recognized, for the first time, the depth of my desire to tell stories. The recurring fantasy of my adolescence was that I would grow up to live in a garret, where I would write brilliant poems and novels. I would not make much money. This went without saying and was the price to be paid for giving my life to art. I did not care about money or possessions. I wanted only the chance to write.

———

We all tell stories. We trade information, get to know each other, provide entertainment, make sense of a senseless world, laugh and cry through the telling of stories. What is gossip, the oldest form of communication, but telling stories? Yet the most significant stories often remain unspoken, hidden away. These are the stories we tell ourselves in the privacy of our own minds and hearts about who we are and who we may become.

The story I was telling myself when I turned thirty and wore my "I forgot to have children" T-shirt around New York was this: I would never meet the right man. This was the year when *Newsweek* magazine came out with an infamous article declaring that a woman who was single at thirty had only a 20 percent chance of ever getting married. The odds were stacked against me, the experts said, and I was inclined to agree with them, not so much because I trusted their forecasting. No, it was more that I wasn't at all sure I wanted to get married.

In this, as in my lack of desire to have a child, I was aware of being distinctly different. My single friends were desperate. They scanned the personals tirelessly and went on a seemingly endless chain of blind dates. They talked about almost nothing else. Consumed with the longing for love and companionship, with the great hope of beginning the adult lives they had imagined, they were also terrified that the time for having children would pass before they found a partner.

One of these friends, a woman named Betsy, showed me a collection of baby clothes she had purchased. She laid the tiny things out on the bed in her studio apartment, darling little knitted sweaters and hats, a miniature pair of denim overalls. She was not seeing anyone at the time and was not planning to get pregnant until she met the right person. The articles of clothing lying there, waiting for a baby to fill them, were heartbreaking.

I felt compassion for Betsy. She was so unhappy, so filled with longing for something she knew should be part of her life but that she could not make happen. At the same time, I was perplexed. I could not imagine going out and buying clothes for a baby that did not show any signs of existing. How could anyone have such a tenacious desire for something so abstract? I understood that to my friends, the husbands they wanted to find and babies they wanted to bear were not the slightest bit abstract, but to me, it all seemed like nothing more than ideas, ideas that did not especially interest me.

Various people questioned me about my single state. Robin, a friend from college, was especially blunt and persistent.

"Don't you want to meet someone?" she asked.

We were sitting at her kitchen table after work one day. Robin had recently been married and wanted everyone to share her bliss.

I shrugged. "Not really."

"Don't you get lonely?"

Yes, I did get lonely, but I did not want to admit to this. It was loneliness that drove me out on occasional dates and led to brief, ill-fated affairs. I shrugged again. "I want to write. I don't see how I can write and be married."

She looked annoyed. "Of course you can write and be married. You think that there's a finite amount of energy, but it's not like that. If you let somebody into your life, you'll have more energy, more to give."

"Maybe," I said, quickly changing the subject.

The truth—and it was a hard truth to acknowledge, to myself or others—was that I was happiest when I was alone, seated at my desk, writing. Everything else in life was simply what came before writing or after it. Going through a day at work, meeting a friend for a movie and dinner, talking with my mother on the phone, taking a run along the river, all of it was simply what I had to do in order to make an appearance of being part of this world and to fill the time between the concentrated bouts of writing. My real life was elsewhere, however: in the pages of my journal and short stories and a fledgling novel.

When I was thirty, the choice seemed clear. I could give myself to the writing, or I could give myself to another person. Robin tried to point out that this story I was telling myself, this story I clung to, justifying my choices, could change, but I scoffed at the idea. I did not understand then that the story I told myself was an evolving one, that nothing, not even my own understanding of myself, would remain fixed as I grew older.

For the better part of a year, my cousin tried to convince me to meet the upstairs tenant in her rambling old house in Newton, Massachusetts. We had so much in common, she said. I resisted until one weekend when I was visiting a snowstorm hit and there was no possibility of going anywhere. "I could call Jim and see if he's home," she said hopefully.

"All right," I said with a certain resignation. What did it hurt to meet someone?

It turned out I was the fifth woman she had introduced to Jim. There he was, in the one-bedroom apartment upstairs, in his thirties, a psychologist with a slim, athletic build and neatly trimmed beard, alone. She couldn't stand it. He had to be perfect for someone.

Jim was, I quickly learned, a gentle man with a quick, sharp sense of humor and wide-ranging insight and knowledge on everything from bluegrass music to geology. He made his own jams and jellies and canned them. He read voraciously—fiction, memoir, history, and philosophy. He owned a cabin in Vermont where he planted a huge vegetable garden. We did, as my cousin had promised, have much in common. Among these things was the fact that neither of us wanted to have children, and it was this knowledge that made it much easier, a year and a half later, to say yes to marriage.

I don't remember when Jim and I had our first conversation on the topic. In my memory, the understanding that he didn't want children was simply there, a part of him I recognized and knew from the start, though of course he must have explained it at some point. I experienced it, at least in retrospect, as an essential piece of his make-up, something I absorbed about him as much as discovered, and was both relieved and the slightest bit disappointed to find. I had harbored a minor hope that, if I was going to meet someone, he would persuade me to have children, making the decision for me. I would wake up one morning and find that I was a mother. I would become like everyone else in the world. But in another part of myself, larger and more certain, there was that overriding sense of relief. I was off the hook. I could give up being alone, but I didn't have to become a parent.

We were both thirty-five and convinced, when we met, that we would never marry. The business of trying to find someone was too messy and discouraging and draining. It was easier to give up the idea altogether. Somewhere around thirty, we had both decided we would remain single. Done with wasting our time on relationships that didn't go anywhere, we were determined not to wade back into those waters unless we thought it would lead to commitment and marriage. Otherwise, it wasn't worth it. We were dubious that the person who could convince us to change our minds would come along and, having made our peace with this, remained more or less content in our independent lives. For me, there was the consuming focus of my writing and the freelance business with which I supported myself. For Jim, there was a demanding career as a psychologist and the clients to whom he gave so much. With the decision to get married, with great trepidation, we traded our old story for a new one.

———

"You probably believe that you've finally met the one other person in the world who was meant for you," the priest said. "This is total nonsense, of course."

We were married in the Episcopal Church and, as part of our preparation, met with the priest for counseling. Had I heard him correctly?

"You could have ended up with countless other people," he went on. "The truth is that before this you weren't ready. You didn't meet the 'right person' because you weren't ready to take this step. Now both of you are ready."

His words were shocking. He was supposed to affirm the great wonder and romance of the step we were about to take. Instead, he threw cold water on it. But I recognized, even as I resisted hearing what he had to say, that he was right. The story we were currently telling, that at our more advanced age, against all odds, we had miraculously found each other, the one intended for each of us, was only part of the truth. There was also the truth that we were both stubborn, independent types, late bloomers who took a long time to come around to being able even to imagine each other, let alone make the decision to accept, and attempt to love, each other.

The transition to being married was not an easy one. Jim and I had to learn to give up some of our coveted independence and control. Saturdays were no longer an oasis of free hours we could spend as we liked, without consulting anyone. What time we went to bed at night made a difference to someone else. Gone were nights of staying up all hours with the lights blazing and music playing. We had to learn to take each other into account in making decisions about everything from what to have for dinner to buying a house. Sometimes I wondered if I would get more writing done if I were still single, if it would all somehow be easier. Eventually I came to see that maybe I would write more as a single person, but the writing would not be as good. Life might be easier, but it would not be as rich. Every once in a while, I think about what might have happened if I hadn't met Jim, and we both hadn't been ready to take that step. The vision of that other life as a single person haunts me. How much I would have missed, how much I would have lost. From Jim and with Jim I have learned so much. There are the simple things that have made my life fuller, like planting and harvesting our own potatoes, and the more profound, like learning to truly love.

No doubt people who have children think the same sorts of thoughts. How much they would have missed without having children, how much more impoverished their lives would be. No doubt they look at those who are childless and pity them for what they don't know they lack. My old friend, Robin, was one of these. I was inching toward forty, with no signs of becoming pregnant, when I visited her, emboldening her to ask the question directly. "Are you and Jim planning to have children?"

"No."

A pained look came over her face. "Are you sure?"

"Yes."

"Before we had kids, I was worried about what would happen with me and John," she said. "I thought I wouldn't be able to love him enough and love the kids. But it's not like that. Having kids only made our love stronger. It magnified the love."

I should have simply agreed with her and said no more, but I felt compelled to defend myself. "I can't make a living and write and be married and have kids. The kids would be too much. I just know this."

She gave me the pained look again. "Think about it."

The connection to our earlier conversation was not lost on me. I had made room in my life for Jim. Why couldn't I make room for children too? This time, though, I was sticking to my story. Without the tug of that longing for children that so many others felt, without any desire on the part of my partner, it simply didn't make sense. Being a mother was not in me. I know in my heart that I would be a resentful mother, that my emotional and psychological make-up are such that it has taken everything I have to produce the writing I have produced. I have struggled to find enough left over to give to a marriage. I doubt there would have been enough left over to give to a child.

A couple of years after Jim and I were married, my sister Leela, the one who gave me the T-shirt, called with the news that she was pregnant. There are three of us in my family, "the Towler girls," as we were known as children. I am the oldest. Marie, the middle sister, has remained single and without children. Leela, eight years my junior and recently married, was looking like the last hope for our parents. To their credit, my parents never pressured any of us either to get married or to have children. I remember my father asking, once, "Have you and Jim decided not to have children?"

When I told him yes, that was the case, he responded, rather cautiously, "I hope you've really considered this. You would make wonderful parents."

This is the refrain we have heard from many people, many times. We would make wonderful parents. I understand why they say this. We both enjoy children and are good at interacting with them. Jim has specialized throughout his career in working with children and adolescents. We are the sort of people who, to outward eyes, "should" have children because we would have so much to give them. I can't dispute this. In another life, one we are not leading, I agree—we would make great parents.

My father did not mention the topic again, and in the years since, has accepted, with graciousness and equanimity, the fact that we are not going to provide him with grandchildren. Now my little sister was stepping up to the plate.

When Leela asked me to be present at the birth of her first child, I was honored. I did not suspect she had an ulterior motive. I flew to Michigan ten days before her due date. It was unlikely the doctor would let her carry the baby to term because Leela is a diabetic. The fetus of a diabetic is apt to gain more weight in the last trimester due to the higher blood sugar levels. This, along with possible complications when a diabetic gives birth, makes doctors wary of letting the baby get too big. We hoped we had timed my arrival for just before the birth.

Leela met me at the airport, waving wanly when I spotted her at the gate. I tried not to show too much surprise at her size. She was huge, her belly so enormous it seemed miraculous that she could walk. In fact, she didn't really walk. It was more like a waddle, shuffling from one foot to the other, trying to balance all that weight on a frame that did not appear designed to hold it.

I went to hug her, but I succeeded in merely draping my arms over her shoulders, unable to get much closer. "You look great," I said, attempting to sound convincing.

"No, I don't. I look like hell and I feel like hell. If this baby isn't born by tomorrow, I'm going to kill myself."

OK, I thought, *so much for the beatific expectant mother I had been imagining.*

"I'm exhausted," Leela said when we reached her house. "I haven't slept in three weeks."

"Why don't you take a nap?" I suggested.

"How can I take a nap when I can't lie down? Or sit for more than ten minutes without having to pee?"

"Why don't you try the couch? I could prop pillows around you."

"Right, like the couch is going to make a difference." She went stomping to the kitchen.

I followed her. "Do you want something to drink?"

"No, I do not want something to drink," she spat. "I want this baby to be born."

Leela's mood did not improve in the days that followed. On the third day of my visit, I accompanied her to her appointment at the hospital clinic. To her great relief, the doctor decided to prepare Leela to be induced, putting a gel on her cervix. The plan was to try this for a few days to see if the contractions would start on their own, but the response was instantaneous. Before long, the contractions were five minutes apart. Leela's husband, David, arrived from work, and we were ushered into a birthing room.

It was clear from the start that I had no business being in that room. Though I knew that Leela had wanted me there to support her and David, and simply to share the experience, I felt helpless and overwhelmed and ill prepared. I had never attended a Lamaze class or seen a film of a birth. I had no idea what to expect and no idea what to do. I had paid little or no attention to the pregnancy and childbirth stories I had heard over the years. I settled for being the one to apply the frequently begged for ChapStick while David said over and over and over, in a remarkably calm and controlled voice, "You're doing just great. OK, breathe in. That's good. Now breathe out."

After more than twenty hours of labor, Leela's cervix had dilated to just eight centimeters. We had gone through a night and the better part of a day without sleep. Though Leela had finally agreed to drugs and an epidural, she was in such pain from the contractions that she was hallucinating, telling me she saw our dead grandmother at the foot of the bed. When I called my father from a payphone out in the hallway to give him an update, I began sobbing the moment I heard his voice, scaring him beyond reason. Every few hours, I went to the vending machines or the cafeteria. David and I ate bagels and cream cheese and candy bars and popcorn. I kept applying ChapStick to Leela's lips and fishing ice chips from a plastic cup for her to suck on. David kept telling her to breathe. When the labor had gone on almost twenty-four hours, the doctor suggested it was time to consider a cesarean section. Leela came out of the haze of pain. "No. Give me more time."

I nearly burst into tears again. I avoided looking at David. Both of us would have done anything to convince her. I was ready to fall on my knees and beg her to have that C-section.

The doctor agreed to give her another half hour to see if she would dilate more. Leela didn't understand, though we tried to explain, that it had been three hours since there had been any change. She thought it was fifteen minutes. The doctor, called away for an emergency C-section, left us alone for far longer than half an hour. The contractions came every minute, wracking her body. In between she fell asleep and snored, only to wake sixty seconds later, moaning and seizing David's hand, her hair plastered to her forehead, wet with sweat. I glanced at the window and saw that darkness was falling. It did not seem possible that we were going to go through a second night of this. Exhaustion and despair filled the air, like a fog surrounding the bed where Leela lay. In her delusional state, Leela was still clinging to the idea of the natural birth she had imagined, but David and I were long past imagining anything but an end to this ordeal. It had come to seem like simply a marathon of suffering. I could barely remember that there was supposed to be a baby at the end of this.

Finally a nurse arrived with two sets of green scrubs for me and David. "Come on," she said. "Rules are only one person in the operating room, but you've been here through all this. I'm getting you both in."

We made a procession down the hall to the operating room and there, at 7:09 p.m., John Towler Kausch was delivered by C-section after twenty-eight hours of labor. He weighed nine pounds and one ounce. David and I stood on either side of Leela, at the head of the gurney. A small plastic curtain was erected so she could not see what was happening below her waist. I could have looked over and watched the procedure, but I chose not to, until they lifted him into the air. He was so big, his arms and legs so long, his head so round, already so very much a person, so very much himself. It was impossible to believe he had been inside my sister's body. Everything about that moment was a glorious and fantastic miracle.

The next day, when I entered the hospital room and saw my sister propped up in bed, cradling Jack in her arms, I felt a tremendous wave of gratitude to Leela for her great act of faith in having a baby. It was as if she had done it for me, though of course she had not.

A few years later, Leela confessed that she had asked me to be there for Jack's birth because she thought it would convince me to have a child. "How did you think that was going to persuade me?" I said, laughing.

"I guess it wasn't the best idea," she said.

I love being an aunt, a role I seem ideally suited to play. Jack, now thirteen years old, sends me the poems he writes and always requests books as birthday gifts, though he does not think he wants to be a writer. He is learning Arabic and wants to be an archaeologist. Eve, his younger sister, plays the harp for me when I visit and demonstrates her ballet positions. She wants to teach music when she grows up. I have watched them go from being infants to toddlers to wonderfully articulate young people. I have shared the wonder and hope with which they have grown, with which they see the world, discovering, through them, that wonder and hope again in myself.

I sometimes think that Jim and I just ran out of time. We weren't ready to have children when we got married, for the obvious reasons we gave and many others, ones we could voice and ones we could not. Now that I am fifty, those reasons seem to matter less. How many books I produce in the course of my career as a writer does not feel as crucial as it once did. I am more focused on the small moments, the simple pleasures that make life what it is. I am still most myself when I am at the desk, writing, but there's everything else I love too—being in Vermont, when Jim and I work in the garden and take long bike rides on back roads, and dinners of good food and wine with friends, and nights out at concerts and plays and movies. There's happiness in all of it. A missed day of writing is not the cause for anxiety, frustration, even anger, that it once was.

There have been times when I revisited the idea of having children, when I asked Jim, "Are you sure?" There have been times when I watched a mother with her daughter, strangers on the street, and thought, *That could be me.* There have been times when my period was late, and I imagined that maybe, surprise of surprises, pregnancy would force us to become parents. There have been times when I listened to older women talk about seeing their children married, about the births of grandchildren, and felt a pang of regret, knowing I will not have those experiences. But these times have been few and far between. For the most part, it has been clear that, though it could have gone another way, this is the way it went for me, and it is right.

There are many ways to tell a given story. This story can be told as one about a choice not made, a path not taken. Framed by a culture where having children is the norm, it is a story about what I did not do. People feel justified asking the question, Why don't you have children? I don't ask them, Why *do* you have children? But I have not experienced this story as one of negation. For me, it is a story of embracing, at each turn in my life, what was best for me and what was best in me.

As a woman, I feel peculiarly compelled to defend my choice not to have children. I shouldn't feel this way. Perhaps just as no one truly makes a decision to have a child—it is too momentous and life-changing an event to be reduced to something that can be debated, pros and cons weighed, a decision arrived at—no one truly decides not to have a child either. It is an evolution in a life as much as it is a decision, a recognition of who you are.

The story I have told, like the stories of many other women, those who have children and those who do not, is a story about accepting ourselves and the vast possibilities afforded by the accident of time and place of birth. It is a story about finding the stories that fit us best. It is a story about growing into the lives we are given.

Katherine Towler is the author of the novels *Snow Island*, *Evening Ferry*, and *Island Light*, a trilogy set on a New England island. She is also coeditor with Ilya Kaminsky of *A God in the House: Poets Talk about Faith*. Her first novel was chosen as a Barnes and Noble Discover Great New Writers title, and she was awarded the George Bennett Fellowship at Phillips Exeter Academy. She teaches in the MFA program in writing at Southern New Hampshire University and lives in New Hampshire.

Story Reflection Questions

1. What is one moment in the story that stayed with you?

   _____

   _____

   _____

2. What questions did you find yourself asking as you read the story?

   _____

   _____

   _____

3. What challenged you about the story?

   _____

   _____

   _____

4. What surprised you about the story?

   _____

   _____

   _____

5. How does this story relate to your own life experience?

   _____

   _____

   _____

Editor Biographies

Kate Cockrill is the Executive Director and co-founder of The Sea Change Program, a non-profit organization dedicated to transforming the culture of stigma around abortion and other stigmatized reproductive experiences. She is a leading researcher conceptualizing and measuring abortion stigma in the United States and around the world. She has authored twelve peer-reviewed, scholarly articles, and her research on stigma has been profiled in the *New York Times*, *Newsweek*, *Salon*, *Slate*, and *RH Reality Check*. She lives with her husband, mother and two children in Albany, California.

Lucia Leandro Gimeno is the Untold Stories Project Manager at The Sea Change Program. He is a trans masculine social worker based in Atlanta, Georgia. They graduated from Columbia University's School of Social Work, where he focused on clinical practice within an anti-oppression framework. He lived in New York City for thirteen years, organizing with queer and trans* communities of color. He was a founding board member of FIERCE and former staff at The Audre Lorde Project. They were part of Ping Chong + Company's *Secret Survivors*, a play about adult survivors of child sexual abuse. A current member of SONG (Southerners On New Ground), a southern regional LGBTQ organization, Lucia Leandro is also a future full-spectrum doula, expert *chilaquiles* maker, fashion queen, movement builder, and listener extraordinaire. Some people say you can even hear his laugh from a mile away.

Steph Herold is the Deputy Director and co-founder of The Sea Change Program. She is an award-winning activist and researcher with a background in abortion care, abortion funds, and reproductive health advocacy. Her writing has been featured in *The Nation*, *RH Reality Check*, *Jezebel*, and *Our Bodies, Ourselves*. Steph is a recognized expert on abortion access, appearing in various media outlets including the *Melissa Harris-Perry Show*.

Campus Progress named Steph one of the top fifteen young feminists, and *Time* magazine profiled her abortion rights activism in January 2013. She served on the board of directors of the New York Abortion Access Fund for three years and currently serves on the ACCESS: Women's Health Justice board of directors. When she's not fighting for abortion rights, you can find her walking around Lake Merritt in Oakland with her husband and their rescue pitbull, Lucky.